FEDERICO GARCÍA

Doña Rosita the Spinster

translated,
with commentary and notes by
GWYNNE EDWARDS

METHUEN DRAMA

Methuen Drama Student Edition

10 9 8 7 6 5 4 3 2 1

This edition first published in the United Kingdom in 2008 by
Methuen Drama
A & C Black Publishers Ltd
38 Soho Square, London W1D 3HB

An earlier version of this translation was published by Methuen Drama in
Lorca Plays: One in 1987; copyright © 1987, 2008 by Gwynne Edwards
and Herederos de Federico García Lorca

Commentary and notes copyright © 2008 by Gwynne Edwards

Doña Rosita la soltera o El lengaje de las flores by Federico Garcia Lorca
copyright © Herederos de Federico Garcia Lorca.

Under the provisions of the Copyright, Designs and Patents Act, 1988,
Herederos de Federico García Lorca and Gwynne Edwards have asserted
their rights to be identified respectively as the authors and translator of the
play and Gwynne Edwards as the author of the Commentary and Notes

A CIP catalogue record for this book is available from the British Library

ISBN 978 1 408 10505 4

Typeset by SX Composing DTP, Rayleigh, Essex
Printed and bound in Great Britain by
CPI Cox & Wyman, Reading, RG1 8EX

Contents

Federico García Lorca: 1898–1936

1898   Born on 5 June 1898 in the village of Fuente Vaqueros
in the province of Granada, the eldest of the four
children of Don Federico García Rodríguez, a wealthy
farmer and landowner, and Doña Vicenta Lorca
Romero, a former schoolteacher in the village.

1907   The family moves to the village of Asquerosa, later
called Valderrubio, only three miles from Fuente
Vaqueros, where Don Federico buys a large house.

1908   Attends a boarding school in the town of Almería,
–09   some seventy miles from Granada, but his stay there is
cut short by illness.

1909   Don Federico moves the family to Granada, the city
which was to play such an important part in Lorca's
work. He attends a small private school, the College of
the Sacred Heart of Jesus, which, despite its name, is
free of clerical influence. He is much more interested in
music, in particular in playing the piano, than in his
academic studies.

1914   After failing the second part of his final secondary
–15   education examination in 1914, he retakes it
successfully in the following year and, at the instigation
of his parents, enters the Faculties of Philosophy and
Letters and of Law at the University of Granada. His
university career proves to be less than remarkable, but
he comes under the influence of two distinguished
professors: Martín Domínguez Berrueta, Professor of
the Theory of Literature and the Arts, and Fernando de
los Ríos Urruti, Professor of Political and Comparative
Law. His musical abilities continue to develop under
the teaching of Don Antonio Segura. He joins the Arts
Club in Granada and also begins to frequent the Café

Alameda, a meeting-place for the intellectuals and
artists of the town, as well as for foreign visitors
such as H. G. Wells, Rudyard Kipling and Artur
Rubinstein.

1916 Study trips in May and October, organised by
Domínguez Berrueta, to various Spanish towns and
cities.

1917 In the spring and summer two further study trips.
Lorca begins to write poetry, prose and short plays.
Much of the poetry is concerned with sexual love and
reveals the conflict in his mind between sexual desire
and Catholic sexual morality.

1918 With the financial assistance of his father, Lorca
publishes *Impressions and Landscapes,* a book based
on his earlier travels with Domínguez Berrueta.

1919 In Granada meets Gregorio Martínez Sierra, a Madrid
theatre producer, who encourages him to write a play
about an injured butterfly (*The Butterfly's Evil Spell*),
and the great Spanish composer, Manuel de Falla, with
whom he begins an influential friendship. Moves from
Granada to Madrid, commencing a ten-year stay at the
Residencia de Estudiantes, an educational institution
based on the Oxbridge college system. Meets Luis
Buñuel, the future film director, who had entered the
Residencia in 1917.

1920 *The Butterfly's Evil Spell* is premiered at the Teatro
Eslava in Madrid on 22 March but closes after four
performances. Audience hostility towards a play about
cockroaches, a butterfly and a scorpion is accompanied
by poor reviews.

1921 Publication in Madrid of Lorca's first volume of poetry,
Book of Poems.

1922 Completes a play for puppets, *The Tragicomedy of
Don Cristóbal and Señorita Rosita.* In February Lorca
lectures on 'deep song' (flamenco song) at the Arts
Club in Granada, and, with Manuel de Falla and
Miguel Cerón, helps to organise the Festival of Deep
Song, held on 13 and 14 of June in the Alhambra's
Plaza de los Aljibes. In anticipation of these events, he
had written in the previous year a series of poems

inspired by 'deep song' which he hoped to publish in conjunction with the festival.

1923 Organises with Manuel de Falla a puppet show which includes Lorca's own puppet play, *The Girl Who Waters the Basil Plant,* and which takes place on 6 January in the García Lorcas' large flat in Granada. In the same month Lorca completes his law degree. In the Residencia he embarks on his important friendship with Salvador Dalí.

1924 Works on a collection of poems, *Gypsy Ballads,* on his second full-length play, *Mariana Pineda,* and on another play strongly influenced by the puppet tradition, *The Shoemaker's Wonderful Wife.* At the Residencia he becomes friendly with Rafael Alberti, who would soon become one of Spain's leading poets.

1925 Stays with Salvador Dalí and his sister, Ana María, at the family homes in Cadaqués and Figueras. Reads *Mariana Pineda* to them. Visits and is much impressed by Barcelona. Back in Granada writes several short plays, of which *Buster Keaton's Spin* and *The Maiden, the Sailor and the Student* survive.

1926 Completes *The Love of Don Perlimplín for Belisa in his Garden.* In Granada he delivers an important lecture, 'The Poetic Image in Don Luis de Góngora', on the great seventeenth-century Spanish poet. Publishes *Ode to Salvador Dalí.*

1927 Premiere of *Mariana Pineda,* to great acclaim, on 24 June at the Teatro Goya in Barcelona. Lorca exhibits twenty-four of his drawings at the Galerías Dalmau in the same city. Publishes *Songs,* his second volume of poems. *Mariana Pineda* opens at the Teatro Fontalba in Madrid on 12 October and is enthusiastically received.

1928 Edits the first issue of the literary magazine, *Cockerel.* He becomes involved with a young sculptor, Emilio Aladrén, to whom he is passionately attracted. At the end of July *Gypsy Ballads* is published to great critical acclaim, but is criticised by Dalí and Buñuel for being too traditional and not sufficiently avant-garde. During the summer Lorca feels depressed. In the autumn he

delivers two lectures to the Athenaeum Club in
Granada, 'Imagination, Inspiration and Escape in
Poetry', and 'Sketch of the New Painting'.

1929   The Madrid premiere of *The Love of Don Perlimplín
for Belisa in his Garden* is banned by the authorities.
On 29 April *Mariana Pineda* opens triumphantly at the
Teatro Cervantes in Granada. Emilio Aladrén begins to
be involved romantically with the English girl he would
marry two years later. This, together with anxieties
about his deteriorating relationship with Dalí and
about his work and his growing fame, exacerbates his
depression. His family decide to send him to New York
in the company of Fernando de los Ríos, where, after
visiting Paris, London, Lucton School near Ludlow,
Oxford, and Southampton, he arrives on 19 June.
Enrols as a student of English at Columbia University,
visits Harlem, then spends the summer in Vermont
before returning to New York. Witnesses the Wall
Street Crash. Works on *Poet in New York* and writes
Trip to the Moon, a screenplay for the silent cinema,
inspired in part by a visit to Coney Island but
expressing too his own sexual anxieties.

1930   Leaves New York for Cuba, arriving in Havana on 7
March. Works on *The Public* and on *Ode to Walt
Whitman.* Returns to Spain at the end of June. *The
Shoemaker's Wonderful Wife* is premiered in Madrid at
the Teatro Español on 24 December.

1931   Publication of *Poem of Deep Song.* Completes *When
Five Years Pass.* Appointed by the new left-wing
Republican government as the artistic director of the
Teatro Universitario, a touring theatre group which
came to be known as 'La Barraca'. For the next four
years the company would perform the great Spanish
plays of the sixteenth and seventeenth centuries in the
towns and villages of rural Spain as part of the
government's broad-based educational programme.

1932   Lorca works on *Blood Wedding.* Reads *Poet in New
York* in Barcelona.

1933   Premiere of *Blood Wedding* on 8 March at the Teatro
Beatriz in Madrid, acclaimed by all the critics. *The*

Love of Don Perlimplín for Belisa in his Garden
premiered at the Teatro Español in Madrid on 5 April.
Lorca works on *Yerma* and in October travels to
Argentina where he both lectures and attends
productions of his own plays, *Blood Wedding* and *The
Shoemaker's Wonderful Wife*, both triumphantly
received in Buenos Aires.

1934 *Mariana Pineda* opens in Buenos Aires on 12 January
but receives only lukewarm reviews. Lorca's adaptation
of Lope de Vega's *The Foolish Lady* is specially
performed for an audience of actors. He arrives in
Spain once again on 11 April and recommences work
with 'La Barraca'. The bullfighter Ignacio Sánchez
Mejías, a close friend of Lorca, receives fatal wounds in
the bullring in Manzanares on 11 August. Shortly
afterwards Lorca begins writing *Lament for Ignacio
Sánchez Mejías* and also works on *Doña Rosita the
Spinster*. On 29 December *Yerma* opens at the Teatro
Español in Madrid. Despite an attempt by the Right to
disrupt the performance, the play is received with great
enthusiasm by both audience and critics.

1935 *The Shoemaker's Wonderful Wife* opens at the Madrid
Coliseum on 18 March. Publication of *Lament for
Ignacio Sánchez Mejías*. *The Puppet Show of Don
Cristóbal* performed in the Paseo de Recoletos during
the Madrid Book Fair. Lorca's version of *The Foolish
Lady* is performed in both Madrid and Barcelona.
Yerma opens in Barcelona on 17 September. Lorca
works on *Sonnets of Dark Love* and on *Play Without a
Title*. *Blood Wedding* opens in Barcelona on 22
November at the Principal Palace Theatre, to be
followed by the triumphant premiere, on 12 December,
of *Doña Rosita the Spinster*.

1936 Increasing political trouble in Spain. The Right and
Centre parties defeated by the left-wing Popular Front
in the February General Election. In the following
months Lorca's socialist sympathies are increasingly in
evidence. Publishes *Six Galician Poems* and *First Songs*.
Works on *The Dreams of My Cousin Aurelia*, *Blood
Has No Voice* (now lost), and *Play Without a Title*.

Rehearsals of *When Five Years Pass* for a production at the Anfistora Club. *The House of Bernarda Alba* is completed on 19 June and in the following week reads the play to groups of his friends. Political unrest continues and Lorca leaves Madrid for Granada on 13 July. Five days later Franco initiates a military uprising against the Madrid government. The military in Granada rise on 20 July. Lorca, fearing the worst, takes refuge in the house of a fellow poet and friend, Luis Rosales. He is taken away from there on 16 August and detained in the Civil Government building. In the early hours of the 18 August he is driven by Francoist thugs to a building outside the village of Viznar, north-east of Granada. From there he is taken by lorry, together with three other men, and shot in the olive groves which cover the slopes above the road to the village of Alfacar. In 1940 the authorities in Granada attempted to conceal the assassination by declaring that Lorca had died 'in the month of August 1936 from war wounds'.

Plot

Act One

Rosita, around twenty years old when the play begins, and engaged to be married to her cousin, lives with her aunt and uncle in the district of Granada known as the Albaicín, not far from the Alhambra. The Uncle spends much of his time cultivating his flowers, in particular his roses, and has recently succeeded in growing the *rosa mutabilis*, a rose which is red in the morning, pale in the evening, and dead by the following day. When Rosita first appears, she is spirited and energetic, and in her rose-coloured dress has all the vibrancy of the *rosa mutabilis* in its early stages. Cherished by her aunt and uncle since the death of her parents, she is also adored by the Housekeeper, the servant who has worked for the family for many years. Rosita's cousin, the Nephew, enters and informs the Aunt that, in spite of his engagement, he is required by his father to return to Argentina in order to work on the family estate, an announcement which leads the Aunt to fear that he will never return. Meanwhile, unaware of this development, Rosita converses with her three friends, the resplendently dressed Manolas who vainly visit the Alhambra in search of love. When they depart, the Aunt informs her of her fiancé's intentions, and in a subsequent farewell Rosita and the Nephew reveal their feelings about his departure. She, despondent about the future, doubts that he will return and sees only sadness ahead. He, in contrast, assures her of his love and promises that he will come back for her. The act concludes with Rosita reading from the book which contains the poem about the *rosa mutabilis* and which ends with the allusion to the flower's petals turning white and starting to fall.

Act Two

Ten years have passed and the Nephew has not returned,
though Rosita still receives his letters and anticipates his
arrival. She is now also courted by other suitors, one of
whom, Mr X, begins Act Two by forcing upon the unwilling
Uncle his views on material progress and the promise of the
early years of the twentieth century. This is followed by a
heated but touching exchange between the Aunt and the
Housekeeper about which of them loves Rosita most. For
Rosita, however, Mr X and her other admirers hold no
interest, because she is still preparing for her marriage to the
Nephew and awaiting the arrival of the postman in the
expectation of good news on her saint's day. Before the
postman appears, Rosita receives a visit from the Mother and
her three spinster daughters, all ridiculously and grotesquely
dressed. They come with greetings and presents for her, and
are soon followed by the two Ayola girls, whose wealth
markedly contrasts with the impoverished spinsters and who
find in their pretentiousness a great source of amusement. The
assembled company then proceeds to recite the popular verses,
'What the Flowers Say', to the piano accompaniment of the
Third Spinster, after which the postman arrives with a letter
for Rosita. Amid general excitement, she reveals that at last
the Nephew has decided that their marriage will take place,
but because he is unable to return to Granada in person, it
will be by proxy, which means that someone will represent
him at the marriage ceremony. Despite the protestations of the
Housekeeper that a marriage by proxy is no marriage at all,
Rosita and her friends are overjoyed by the news and begin to
dance in celebration of the forthcoming wedding. Even though
the Uncle has just accidentally cut his only *rosa mutabilis*, its
still bright red colour seems to match the exuberant mood.

Act Three

Ten more years have passed and the circumstances of Rosita's
family are greatly changed. The Uncle has been dead for six
years and, having failed to repay the mortgage on the house as
a result of his spending on his flowers and his generosity to

others in financial straits, has left the Aunt with no other option but to sell the family home and move to a smaller property. The Aunt is dispirited and physically less well. Furthermore, in spite of the Housekeeper's efforts to cheer her up, her despondency is deepened by the recent discovery that Rosita's fiancé has been married for the past eight years to an Argentinian girl but has continued to keep alive her niece's hopes. Don Martín enters to pay a farewell call and while he is there the removal men start to take away the furniture. An ageing and crippled bachelor, he teaches at a local school where he and his colleagues are mocked by the pupils. He laments both their cruel behaviour and his own failure to achieve the success as a writer which he has always craved. As for Rosita, she reveals that, although she has known for a while of her fiancé's abandonment of her, she has continued to hope against hope, but is now resigned to her fate, accepts that everything has changed, that her friends are married, and that she, a spinster, has become an object of mockery. Visits from the son of the eldest Manola, who is now dead, and then from the Third Spinster, are further reminders of the passage of time. Rosita, now dressed in white and as pale as the *rosa mutabilis*, leaves the empty house, accompanied by her ageing aunt and the Housekeeper.

Commentary

Lorca and the theatre of his time

Lorca's dozen or so full-length plays, written during a
relatively short period of sixteen years, reveal a great variety
of influences, both Spanish and foreign. As far as European
theatre in the first quarter of the twentieth century was
concerned, there was among dramatists and practitioners who
wished to see the theatre flourish and progress a clear reaction
against the Naturalist movement of the nineteenth century.
This, roughly speaking, was a scientific approach which
emphasised heredity and environment as the key 'determining'
factors in the lives of human beings, and which, in the theatre,
led dramatists to attempt to recreate in their plays the here-
and-now of everyday reality, in which both individuals and
groups of people are shown to be influenced less by their own
desires and aspirations than by those external pressures. In
addition, and precisely because it emphasised the similarities
rather than the differences between people, Naturalism in the
theatre created a social levelling of the classes presented on
stage, and blurred both the distinctions between the 'high' and
the 'low', the 'serious' and the 'comic', and those individual
moments in a play which are 'dramatic' or 'undramatic'. The
influence of Naturalism can be seen quite clearly in the plays
of Anton Chekhov (1860–1904) and Henrik Ibsen
(1828–1906), though both dramatists were, of course,
responsive to other movements in the theatre.

Directly opposed to Naturalism, with its emphasis on the
material world, was Symbolism, which was concerned with
the transcendental, the greater reality which lies beyond the
mundane world in which we live, and which had been
anticipated in the nineteenth century in the theory and
practice of such men as Richard Wagner. In his music drama
Wagner had attempted to evoke through archetypal characters
and by means of a theatrical technique which combined

music, poetry, acting and stage design those eternal truths
which lie beyond the visible world. As far as twentieth-century
theatre is concerned, it was the Belgian dramatist Maurice
Maeterlinck (1862–1949) who led the way. In *The Blue Bird,*
written in 1905, two children, Tyltyl and Mytyl, embark on a
quest to find the Blue Bird which will cure the sick child of a
neighbour, are guarded by Light but obstructed by Night, and
the Blue Bird escapes. The characters are clearly not so much
individuals set in a particular time and space, as would have
been the case in Naturalist drama, but archetypal beings who
embody the very essence of human aspiration, struggle and
ultimate failure, the symbolic nature of the characters and the
stage action underpinned by stage design and movement
which is highly stylised. In European theatre as a whole the
same movement away from Naturalism was to be found in the
theory and practice of such significant stage designers and
directors as Adolphe Appia, Edward Gordon Craig and Max
Reinhardt, all of whom favoured symbolical representation
and a close integration of the different elements of
performance in order to stir the imagination of an audience.

The early years of the twentieth century were also marked
by the development of other significant movements in the
Arts, such as Cubism, Futurism, Dadaism, Expressionism, and
later on, in the 1920s, Surrealism. In their different ways they
are movements which represent both a rejection of hitherto
accepted values and ideals, and an attempt to find new ways
of looking at the world. Expressionism, dating from about
1910, was given an added impulse by the terrible atrocities of
the 1914–18 war and was often concerned, therefore, with
positive values such as the creation of an equal and just
society and the rejection of the machine age in favour of a
more simple society. In order to communicate its message
Expressionist theatre, in the hands of dramatists such as Ernst
Toller and Georg Kaiser, employed exaggeration and
distortion in both characterisation, language and staging.

Surrealism, associated in particular with the Paris
Surrealists of the 1920s but evident before that, was
concerned in part with the unconscious mind, with the inner
rather than the outer man, with the illogical and the
irrational, and with the expression of feelings and emotions

uncontrolled by reason. In the theatre of France, in plays such as *The Breasts of Tiresias* and *Parade,* both performed in 1917, Guillaume Apollinaire and Jean Cocteau set out to undermine the Naturalist tradition in order to suggest both the importance of the unconscious mind and the truth that lies beneath the appearance of things. In consequence, the technique of the plays lies at the very opposite extreme to Naturalism, employing all manner of exaggeration and distortion to evoke a world in which logic plays no part.

In Spain itself Naturalism had its equivalent in writers such as Benito Pérez Galdós (1843–1920), who, apart from being Spain's greatest novelist of the nineteenth century, also wrote twenty-two plays, and Jacinto Benavente (1866–1954), who dominated the Spanish theatrical scene for many years. Both Galdós and Benavente reacted against the inflated neo-Romantic style which had characterised the theatre in the latter part of the nineteenth century, and both were concerned in their own plays with more realistic characters, background and language. This said, the theatre of Benavente did not change or evolve very much during his long career. Having discovered a successful formula, he largely settled for it, and in his hands, as well as in the hands of a number of other successful and popular dramatists, Spanish theatre remained for many years rather stagnant and undemanding.

Of the dramatists who, influenced by cultural trends outside Spain, attempted to advance the cause of Spanish theatre through bold experiment, the most important figure before Lorca was undoubtedly Ramón del Valle-Inclán (1866–1936). His early work, in particular *The Savage Plays,* reveals the clear influence of European Symbolism, for it is concerned, in its portrayal of the history of Don Juan Manuel Montenegro and his family, with the evocation of timeless and universal issues, above all good and evil and the redemption of Man through suffering. Valle-Inclán's technique, moreover, is highly reminiscent in its synthesis of stage settings, costumes, movement, lighting and dialogue of the ideas on theatre of Symbolist stage designers and producers such as Adolphe Appia and Edward Gordon Craig.

By 1920, and partly in response to the horrors of the First

World War, Valle-Inclán's Symbolist phase had given way to
his theory and practice of the grotesque, *esperpentismo,* an
approach to dramatic writing which is defined in *Bohemian
Lights,* written in 1920, which owes something to
Expressionism, as well as to the puppet tradition, and which
Valle-Inclán believed more appropriate to the expression of
the absurd and grotesque nature of Spanish life as he saw it.
Other significant writers of the time who turned their back on
Naturalism were Miguel de Unamuno (1864–1936), whose
stark, unadorned plays often exteriorise emotional and
intellectual conflicts, and Jacinto Grau (1877–1958), whose
work after 1918 expresses the preoccupations of that time in a
style which closely integrates the different elements of stage
performance.

As far as Spain is concerned, mention must be made too of
the important centuries-old tradition of puppet-theatre and
farce. Cervantes, for example, had introduced a puppet show,
Master Peter's Puppet Show, into the second part of *Don
Quixote,* published in 1615, while the same year also saw the
appearance of a collection of eight short plays, *Interludes,*
which in their presentation of ingenious situations and boldly
comic characters were models of their kind. Valle-Inclán in his
grotesque plays, Jacinto Grau in *Mr Pygmalion,* written in
1921, and Carlos Arniches (1866–1943) in his *grotesque
farces,* continued that tradition in the first two decades or so
of the twentieth century.

Lorca's first play, *The Butterfly's Evil Spell,* reveals the very
clear influence of Symbolism, as well as, in all probability, the
direct influence of Maeterlinck's *The Blue Bird.* Through the
story of Curianito, the young cockroach who falls in love with
the Butterfly but is rejected by her, Lorca explores the themes
of love, frustration and death which are so central to his own
existence. This, moreover, is enhanced by Lorca's highly
stylised presentation of the characters and events which
transforms the particularity of the onstage action into a
visual metaphor with which we can all identify. There are
strong elements of Symbolism too in Lorca's second play,
Mariana Pineda, despite the fact that the subject is historical
and, to that extent, more 'realistic'. Once more the themes are
the characteristic Lorca themes of passion and frustration,

but, as well as this, the purity of Mariana herself is set against the evil of Pedrosa, the Chief of Police, while the conflict between them, itself universal in its implications, is set within an essentially poetic and symbolic frame, created by the white of walls and costume, the black of Pedrosa's clothes, and the approach of night. The concerns of Symbolism, including concepts of staging which are strictly anti-naturalistic, are to be found throughout Lorca's theatre.

At the same time, his interest in puppet-theatre was evident from early on. In 1922, two years after the disastrous opening of *The Butterfly's Evil Spell,* he completed a play for puppets, *The Tragicomedy of Don Cristóbal and Señorita Rosita,* and in the following year organised a puppet show in Granada with Manuel de Falla. It was an aspect of his work which was, in conjunction with farce, to become more important in the years ahead, for between 1924 and 1935 *The Shoemaker's Wonderful Wife, The Love of Don Perlimplín for Belisa in his Garden,* and *The Puppet Play of Don Cristóbal* were all written and performed.

Lorca's interest in this tradition and his championing of it in his own work is easily explained, for, like Symbolism, puppet-theatre and farce are anti-naturalistic, characterised by a simplicity and a boldness which allowed Lorca that freedom of expression, that spontaneity and vitality which he believed to be the essential ingredients of a living theatre. So, in the prologue to *The Puppet Play of Don Cristóbal* he refers to 'the delicious and hard language of the puppets', and later the director of the play itself wishes to 'fill the theatre with fresh wheat', a clear pointer to the stale Naturalism of much contemporary Spanish theatre. Although the characters of *The Shoemaker's Wonderful Wife* are played by actors, the technique is very much that of the puppet play as they engage in vigorous physical and verbal action against settings which in their boldness echo the immediacy of the characters. They are features of Lorca's theatrical style which, in varying degrees, are to be seen in all his plays.

Surrealism came into its own in Lorca's work in two major plays, *The Public* and *When Five Years Pass,* completed in 1930 and 1931 respectively, though its influence is evident both before and after these particular plays. Lorca's

friendships with Luis Buñuel and Salvador Dalí proved crucial
in relation to the dramatist's familiarity with 'avant-garde'
movements in European culture, as well as to his exposure to
the theories of Sigmund Freud, much read at the Residencia de
Estudiantes in the 1920s. There are clear surrealist elements in
the short piece, *Buster Keaton's Spin,* written in 1925, but it
was the emotional crisis of 1929 which led Lorca to express
his true inner anguish in two full-length and enormously
ambitious plays. In both *The Public,* his only overtly gay play,
and *When Five Years Pass,* arguably his most accomplished
and striking piece of theatre, Lorca's personal obsessions –
love, frustration, passing time and death – are expressed
through an action which is essentially dreamlike, in which the
characters are seen to be echoes of or contrasts to each other
and in which their unconscious fears frequently assume
frightening external forms. Thus, at a crucial moment in Act
One of *When Five Years Pass,* the onstage characters of the
Young Man, the Old Man, the Friend and the Second Friend
are suddenly confronted by a nightmarish scene involving the
Dead Child and the Dead Cat which exteriorises the deep-
seated anxieties of all the onlookers. Greatly influenced by
Surrealism, both plays also reveal in their strongly visual
character and in their fluid movement the imprint of
Symbolism, Expressionism, puppet-theatre and cinema. Once
more Lorca shows himself to be a constant experimenter in
his search for freedom of expression, a fundamental aspect of
his work which is also evident in his screenplay of 1929, *Trip
to the Moon.*

These various influences come together as well, of course, in
Lorca's great plays of the 1930s, including the so-called 'rural
trilogy' of *Blood Wedding, Yerma,* and *The House of
Bernarda Alba.* In one sense, plays whose subjects, characters
and settings are located in the Spanish countryside suggest
Naturalism rather than any kind of stylisation, but in fact the
opposite is true, despite the fact that *Blood Wedding* and *The
House of Bernarda Alba* have their origins in real-life events.
In the first place, the names which Lorca gives his characters
have, for the most part, a generic and archetypal quality: in
Blood Wedding the Mother, the Father, the Bridegroom, the
Bride, the Wife, the Neighbour; in *Yerma* the Pagan Woman,

the First Girl, the Second Girl. And even when there are real names they often have a symbolic resonance: in *Blood Wedding* the two halves of Leonardo's name suggest a 'burning lion'; and in *The House of Bernarda Alba,* the surname Alba has associations with 'dawn' and therefore 'brightness' and 'light', while the connections of Angustias with anguish and Martirio with martyrdom are evident enough. In addition, Lorca's constant linking of the characters of these plays to the soil, the trees, the heat, water, the seasons, in short to the world of nature, creates a very strong sense of their universality. In the final acts of *Blood Wedding* and *Yerma,* moreover, the effect is enhanced and a sense of timelessness created by the appearance of non-human figures: in the former Moon and Death (the Beggar Woman); in the latter the fertility figures of Male and Female. Lorca's use of poetry in both plays, and especially in *Blood Wedding,* also has the effect of universalising the particular through suggestive metaphor, while his suggestions for staging – stark, stylised settings, dramatic lighting effects, and bold movement, including dance – reveal an intention at the opposite extreme from Naturalism. And even if, in *The House of Bernarda Alba,* the poetry of the other two plays is pared away and there seems to be a greater realism, a closer examination suggests that Lorca's predilection is still for an overall stylisation. Indeed, in their different ways the three plays of the rural trilogy can be seen to combine elements of Symbolism, Expressionism, Surrealism, and the puppet tradition, all fused into an anti-naturalistic style of which he increasingly proved to be a master.

Doña Rosita the Spinster, completed between *Yerma* and *The House of Bernarda Alba*, is in many respects different in character from both. Not only does it have a largely urban rather than a rural setting, but it also evokes a period well in the past. Nevertheless, the stylisation which distinguishes those and other Lorca plays is also evident here. Many of the characters have the generic names which partly give his work its sense of universality: the Aunt, the Uncle, the Housekeeper, the Spinsters, the Nephew, the Youth. Furthermore, the link which is established throughout the play between the rose which blooms bright red at noon but quickly fades, and

Rosita, whose beauty and hopes of marriage are slowly
eroded by passing time, creates not only that connection
between human beings and the world of Nature, as is the case
in the rural plays, but also encapsulates a symbolism with
which we can all identify.

The real-life sources of *Doña Rosita the Spinster*

Although *Blood Wedding* and *Yerma*, first performed in
1933 and 1934 respectively, were firmly grounded in reality,
neither of them, nor indeed the later *The House of Bernarda
Alba*, reflected a particular place, drew upon individuals
whom Lorca knew, or contained such personal and
autobiographical elements as did *Doña Rosita the Spinster*,
premiered in Barcelona on 12 December 1935. It is a play
which Lorca described in its rather elaborate title as 'A poem
of Granada in 1900', and which therefore evokes the city to
which the Lorca family had moved from rural Asquerosa
when he was eleven years old, and which exercised a
profound influence on his life thereafter. Granada had also
provided the background to *Mariana Pineda*, completed in
1923 and first performed in 1927, a play set in the first half of
the nineteenth century, in which Lorca dramatised the
historical accounts of the young woman's involvement with
the city's revolutionary liberals, and her subsequent arrest and
execution. The emphasis here, however, is on a Granada
which is dark and ominous, enveloped in wind and rain, and
allusions in the text are mainly to the city's central area: the
Puerta Real, the Bibarrambla Square, the Zacatín, all near the
cathedral. In contrast, the focus in *Doña Rosita* is on the
higher part of the city. Rosita and her aunt and uncle live in
the Albaicín, the district to the north of the Alhambra,
characterised by its steep, labyrinthine streets and its houses
and villas with beautiful enclosed gardens. Close by, the
Alhambra, the greatest Arabic monument in western Europe,
stands on the Sabica Hill, dominating the whole of Granada
and looking outwards towards the rich agricultural plain
known as La Vega and the 11,000-foot-high Sierra Nevada,
which isolates the city from the sea to the south. Both the

Alhambra and the Albaicín were places which Lorca knew intimately during his teenage years and his adult life. But if he sought to evoke them as they had been at the beginning of the twentieth century, it is perfectly clear that the Granada of the play, as well as the character of its inhabitants, was also coloured by Lorca's experience of them in later life.

From the moment his family settled there, Granada's mixture of Christian, Moorish and gypsy culture was for Lorca a source of endless fascination. The Alhambra, built by the city's Moorish rulers during the thirteenth and fourteenth centuries, was in his opinion a supreme example of a sophisticated and highly artistic civilisation which came to an end with the triumph of the Christian armies over the Moors in 1492 and their later expulsion from Spain. In an interview published on 10 June 1936 in the Madrid newspaper *El Sol*, Lorca expressed his opinion in no uncertain fashion: 'It [the Christian victory] was a disaster, even if the opposite view is stated in schools. An admirable civilisation, and a poetry, architecture and sensitivity unique in the world – all were lost . . .' He admired in particular the attention to detail and the beautiful design manifest in the intricate arabesques of the Alhambra and of other Moorish buildings in Granada. He loved too the Moors' cultivation of flowers and plants, of which the Alhambra's Generalife Gardens, with their colourful blooms and babbling water, are a fine example. And he enthused too about Arab-Andalusian poetry, which he was able to read in translation in various anthologies and which influenced some of his own poems.

Lorca's contact with the Alhambra was both frequent and stimulating. In 1922 he and various other influential people, including the celebrated composer Manuel de Falla, organised the flamenco singing competition, the Festival of Deep Song ('Cante jondo') in the Alhambra's Plaza de los Aljibes (the Square of the Wells). He often visited the Alhambra with his friends and knew the guitarist Angel Barrios, who lived in the grounds; he recited his poems from various vantage points; and he delighted, above all, in going to the Alhambra at night, when the effect of moonlight on the beautiful architecture, on the trees, and on water, created a mood of magic and romance which had captivated writers, musicians and painters over many years.

Although the Alhambra had fallen into a gradual decline in the eighteenth and nineteenth centuries in particular, this did not prevent creative artists and educated individuals from investing their descriptions of it with exotic overtones. In *The Adventures of the Last Abencerraje (Les Aventures du dernier Abencérage)*, published in 1826, the French writer François René de Chateaubriand channelled into fictional form his own assignation in the Alhambra with Nathalie de Noailles, describing it in suitably romantic language:

> As the moon rose, its fitful light spread through the empty halls and abandoned courts of the Alhambra. Its beams threw patterns on the grassy lawn, on the walls of the great rooms and their ancient tracery, on the arches of the courtyards, on the moving shadows of the water and the shrubs stirred by the breeze. A nightingale sang in a cypress-tree that grew through the dome of a ruined mosque, and the echoes repeated its sad song.

In 1832 the American, Washington Irving, published his influential *The Alhambra*, followed in 1851 by a revised and enlarged edition. In spite of his criticism of the neglect into which the Alhambra had fallen and of the disreputable individuals who now sought refuge within its walls, Irving, like Chateaubriand before him, was often susceptible to its magic:

> All was open, beautiful; everything called up pleasing and romantic fantasies; Lindaraxa once more walked in her garden; the gay chivalry of Moslem Granada once more glittered about the Court of the Lions! Who can do justice to a moonlight night in such a climate and such a place?[1]

Similarly, the English high Tory, Richard Ford, though essentially practical and down-to-earth in his descriptions of the Alhambra in his *Handbook for Travellers in Spain*, first published in 1844, sometimes lapsed into exotic fantasy:

> But to understand the Alhambra, it must be lived in [. . .] On a

[1] Washington Irving, *Complete Works: The Alhambra*, Boston, Desmond, 1899, p. 69.

stilly summer night all is again given up to the past and to the
Moor; then, when the moon, Diana's bark [sic] of pearl, floats
above it in the air like his crescent symbol, the tender beam
heals the scars [of the Alhambra's decline] . . .[1]

The portrayal of the Alhambra as a mysterious, exotic and
romantic place was, of course, reinforced by many other
writers, as well as by musicians and painters in the course of
the nineteenth and early twentieth centuries. Debussy's
Lindaraja, a work for two pianos, appeared in 1901 and was
inspired by the story of the Moorish princess who lived in the
Alhambra, while *La puerta del vino*, published in 1913 in the
second book of *Préludes*, stemmed from a picture postcard of
the well-known Moorish gateway. Among Spanish composers,
Manuel de Falla completed in 1916 his work for piano and
orchestra, *Nights in the Gardens of Spain* (*Noches en los
jardines de España*), whose first movement evokes the gardens
of the Generalife, and in June of that year he played the piano
part at a concert in the nearby palace of Charles V. The
British artists David Roberts and Frederick Lewis made
sketches, paintings, and lithographs of many aspects of the
Alhambra's buildings, while the exotically named Isidore
Severin Justin Baron de Taylor published a small collection of
the most beautiful coloured lithographs with mysterious and
exotic figures set against the wonderful architecture of the
palaces.

Lorca's evocation of the Alhambra in Act One of *Doña
Rosita* clearly draws both on his personal experience and on
the image of it handed down by the writers, painters and
musicians whose works preceded him. Rosita's account of the
Manolas' visit emphasises darkness ('Oh, how dark the
Alhambra is!'), mystery ('Mysterious muslins move'),
shadowy figures ('Amongst the trees are hidden/Men who
could give them love'), the sound of running water ('the
leaping fountain'), the whisper of the breeze ('the breeze softly
sings'), the dream of love ('The eyes of . . . The youngest [girl]
half-closed in dream'), and the quick glimpse of lace petticoats
('A girl displays a pretty shoe/Through petticoats of lace'). If,

[1] Richard Ford, *A Handbook for Travellers in Spain*, reprinted London,
Centaur Press, 1966, p. 570.

in writing these beautiful lines, he recalled his visits to the
Alhambra on moonlit nights, Lorca also invested Rosita's
account with the romantic associations which colour
Chateaubriand's description of the meeting of two lovers,
Washington Irving's suggestion of a beautiful Moorish girl
walking in her garden, and Taylor's portrayal of exotic figures
against the background of the palaces. Nothing could be
further removed from the spare and austere style of *The
House of Bernarda Alba*, completed a year after *Doña Rosita*.

The Albaicín, with its steep, winding streets, its
whitewashed houses, and its clear evidence of its Moorish
origins – Arabic baths, remnants of mosques, gardens replete
with flowers – was also for Lorca a place of mystery and
exoticism. In an early prose work, *Impressions and
Landscapes* (*Impresiones y paisajes*), published in 1918, he
had described it in the following way:

> The streets are narrow, dramatic flights of steps which are
> amazing and decayed, waving tentacles which wind wearily and
> whimsically and lead to small openings from which can be seen
> the mighty snow-covered peaks of the sierra or the fine and
> clear harmony of the plain. In some places the streets are paths
> full of fear and anguish, flanked by walls over which appear
> clumps of jasmine, climbers, St. Francis rose-bushes. One can
> hear the barking of dogs and distant voices calling out to
> someone in a sensual but disillusioned manner. Other streets
> spill downhill, impossible to descend, full of huge stones, of
> walls eaten away by time, and tragic women are seated there,
> mad women who stare provocatively . . .

The strong feeling of decay and anguish suggested by such a
description encapsulated his feeling of regret that a once great
civilisation had disappeared.

On the other hand, he was enchanted by the villas with
beautiful gardens in the Albaicín, which are known as
'carmenes', of which the house in which Rosita lives with her
aunt and uncle is a fine example. Cultivated originally by the
Arabs, for whom the garden was an image of paradise, the
enclosed garden of a 'carmen' possesses an abundance of
flowers and trees, as well as a fountain, and usually, in the
steep Albaicín, a wonderful view. In this respect, we should

note that, when Rosita, her aunt, and the Housekeeper are obliged to abandon the house in which they have lived for many years and where the Uncle once attended lovingly to his flowers, the smaller house to which they move at the end of the play is said to have 'quite a nice view'. Lorca was, of course, a frequent visitor to those villas owned by his friends in the Albaicín, observing on one occasion that, if he were to live permanently in the city, he would do so only in a 'carmen', 'close to what one feels deeply'. In this context it is worth mentioning too that, although Manuel de Falla did not live in the Albaicín, he had a 'carmen' with a lovely garden in the street known as Antequerela Alta, close to the Alhambra, where Lorca was a frequent visitor.

Familiarity with the gardens of the Generalife and the 'carmenes' does not mean, however, that Lorca had extensive knowledge of the names and species of flowers which grew there. While his work in general alludes to flowers such as roses, geraniums, dahlias and jasmine, *Doña Rosita* required much more specialised knowledge, for the Uncle is able to reel off lists of flowers, and the song sung around the piano in Act Two, 'What the Flowers Say', contains a great variety of flowers together with the feelings and emotions which they symbolise. The story of the *rosa mutabilis*, which changes from red to white in the course of a single day and which is described in the poem read by the Uncle in Act One, was, according to Lorca, contained in a seventeenth-century book about roses and was told to him in 1924 by his friend José Moreno Villa. In 1935 Lorca visited Seville, where he stayed with Joaquín Romero Murube, keeper of the Arabic palace known as the Alcázar, and where he undoubtedly discussed with the gardeners the nature and variety of the flowers cultivated in its beautiful gardens. As for the list of flowers mentioned in the song, Francisco García Lorca has stated that Lorca consulted journals, books and almanacs from the early part of the twentieth century, that he saw such material lying on his desk at the Huerta de San Vicente, the family home in Granada where the play was written, and that the list might have been provided by Emilia Llanos, a close friend. At all events, as in the case of the Alhambra and the Albaicín, Lorca's sources were firmly grounded in reality.

As far as the characters of the play are concerned, many had their origins in people Lorca knew personally. In 1918, for example, he had written a poem called 'Elegy' which was inspired by a young unmarried woman in Granada, Maravillas Pareja, in whose fate Rosita's future was already mirrored:

> In your white hands
> You bear the thread of your illusions,
> Dead for ever, and in your soul
> A passion hungry for kisses of fire . . .

Lorca's cousin, Clotilde García Picossi, might well have been another source, for, just as in the play Rosita's fiancé departs for Argentina, leaving her behind, Clotilde's fiancé, Máximo Delgado García, who had formerly lived in the same village as the Lorca family, and whom Lorca later met, had also abandoned her and gone to live in Argentina. But perhaps the most influential real-life source was Emilia Llanos Medina, who lived with her sister near the Alhambra. Lorca had first met her when he was twenty and, although she was ten years older, had immediately been attracted by both her considerable physical beauty and her intellectual and literary interests. He dedicated three of his books to her: *Impressions and Landscapes*, *Book of Poems* (*Libro de poemas*) and *First Gypsy Ballads* (*Primer Romancero gitano*). He gave her or lent her books by other writers, including Ibsen, Oscar Wilde and Maeterlinck. They frequently went for walks in the Alhambra and the gardens of the Generalife and wrote to each other when Lorca was away from Granada. But, given Lorca's homosexual inclinations, and indeed his sexual confusion in his late teenage years and his early twenties, the relationship with Emilia was never sexual. On the other hand, she might have entertained hopes that their friendship might develop into something more, but Lorca's untimely death in 1936 when Emilia was forty-eight years of age clearly ended what hopes she might have had. For the rest of her life she remained a spinster, keeping a photograph of Lorca in her sitting room, no doubt sadly remembering someone whom she came to regard as her lost love. For his part, he might well have been aware of his failure to reciprocate her feelings and of his part in condemning her to the kind of life which he observed and sympathised with in many other unmarried Spanish women, and which he would embody so touchingly in Rosita. Finally, quite apart from the theme of spinsterhood, there appear to be in Rosita certain echoes of Lorca's mother's life before her marriage. In 1890 Vicenta Lorca, like Rosita, would have been twenty years of age. Furthermore, on account of her father's death before she was born, Vicenta and her mother had been obliged for financial reasons to move house on several occasions, once from a villa not unlike Rosita's 'carmen' to a lesser property. In writing the third act of the play, Lorca might well have recalled his mother's difficult early life, though subsequently, through sheer hard work, she became successful and married one of the richest landowners in Fuente Vaqueros, the birthplace in 1898 of the future poet and dramatist.

Several of the play's other female characters are similarly based on real people. The Housekeeper, one of Lorca's most brilliantly drawn characters, is modelled on many servants he had known, but in particular on Dolores Cuesta, a down-to-earth, outgoing and garrulous woman who had been his wetnurse in Fuente Vaqueros, who worked for the Lorca family for many years, and of whom Lorca himself was particularly fond. Again, Emilia Llanos's servant, Dolores Cebrián, though younger than Dolores Cuesta, was equally earthy and garrulous, was certainly the model for the Wife in *The Shoemaker's Wonderful Wife* (*La zapatera prodigiosa*), and might have been in Lorca's mind as he wrote the later play. As for some of the other female characters, the episode of the three Manolas in Act One derives in part from a popular song but is also based on three real girls who lived on the Cuesta de Gomérez, the steep hill which leads to the Alhambra from the Plaza Nueva in the heart of Granada.

Several of the play's male characters were also based on real people. In Act Three, the schoolteacher, Don Martín, who comes to visit the Aunt and Rosita before they move house, was modelled in part on Martín Scheroff y Aví, a teacher at the College of the Sacred Heart of Jesus, which Lorca had attended from the age of eleven to seventeen. Like the character in the play, Martín Scheroff y Aví taught Literature and Rhetoric. He was an elderly man who, in order to make himself look younger, dyed his hair and moustache, and, just as the fictional character has literary aspirations, so his real-life predecessor published a collection of short stories, together with poems and theatre reviews which appeared in local magazines, all written in a high-flown and outmoded style. A bachelor living on his own, he was also, like the teacher in the play, the object of his pupils' frequent practical jokes. He did not, however, write a play called *Jephthah's Daughter*, of which, even though it was never performed, Lorca's character is extremely proud. In this respect the dramatist was thinking of Antonio Segura Mesa, his elderly music teacher from around 1909 until his death in 1916, who had composed a one-act opera called *The Daughters of Jephthah* which was performed but booed off the stage at its premiere. Even so, given the fact that he provided Lorca with a sound musical education and that the dramatist greatly admired him, it was appropriate that eighteen years after the old man's death, certain aspects of his life, together with those of Martín Scheroff y Aví, should have found their way into the character of the play's Don Martín. In the course of his conversation with the Aunt and Rosita, Don Martín also refers to another teacher who was the butt of the schoolchildren's jokes – a Mr Consuegra, 'a most wonderful Latin teacher'. He too is based on a teacher of the same name at the College of the Sacred Heart of Jesus. And finally, there is Mr X, the professor of Political Economy who at the beginning of Act Two declares his amorous interest in Rosita and proceeds to give the Uncle a highly pompous lecture on the progressive nature of the beginning of the twentieth century. It has been suggested that he is modelled on the real-life Ramón Guixé y Mexía and, to a lesser extent, the distinguished writer and philosopher José Ortega y Gasset, who sat on the board of the Residencia de Estudiantes in Madrid where in the 1920s Lorca lived while attending the university.

There are, in addition, allusions to other individuals and families who do not appear as characters in the play but who were important in Granada society. In Act Two, for example, the Housekeeper sarcastically refers to the father of the two

Ayola girls as 'the high and mighty Ayola, photographer to
His Majesty the King', a position which this individual did
indeed hold, while Francisco García Lorca has stated that
there were numerous photographs in the Lorca household
which bore the name 'Ayola, Photographer'. And again, the
Third Spinster pretentiously claims that she and her sisters
often meet up with 'the Ponce de León girls, or the Herrastis',
both prominent families and part of Granada's gentry during
Lorca's childhood. Indeed, the Pérez de Herrasti family lived
high up in the Albaicín, in a large house beside the present-
day Archaeological Museum.

   While many of the play's places and characters have their
basis in both past and present reality, it dramatises, too, many
of the personal problems which formed the day-to-day reality
of Lorca's life. The theme of passing time had already been to
the fore in earlier plays, but for the dramatist at thirty-seven
years of age the matter must have seemed more pressing than
ever. In the summer of 1931 he had completed *When Five
Years Pass*, significantly subtitled *A Legend of Time*. In Act
One its protagonist, the Young Man, dreams of meeting up
with the Girlfriend in five years' time, but when he finally
does so, she has changed and he is rejected. In the same act,
the Friend desperately attempts to enjoy the moment but,
before he can do so, finds that it has passed him by: 'I've no
time. No time for anything. Everything's rushing by . . . I'm
too late. It's frightening. Always the same. No time.' Rosita's
haste in Act One, as she rushes in and out of the house, is very
similar, while the Housekeeper's description of her
immediately brings to mind the Friend's comment on passing
time: 'Rush, rush, rush. Everything at top speed. She'd prefer
today to be the day after tomorrow. She's off like a shot, here
one minute, gone the next.' Again, in Act One of *When Five
Years Pass*, the Second Friend envisages with horror the
physical changes which come with the passing years and
which he sees before him in the person of the Old Man: 'I
don't want to be all wrinkles and aches like you. I want to live
what's mine to the full and they're taking it away from me.'
Similarly, in Act Three of *Doña Rosita*, the once lively and
beautiful Rosita is well aware of how she has changed over
twenty years and of the physical decline which lies ahead: 'I

know . . . my back [will be] more bent with every passing day. What's happened to me has happened to thousands of others.' If we compare photographs of Lorca himself at the age of twenty with those taken in the last few years of his life, when he was approaching forty, it is perfectly clear that the slim attractive and rather romantic young man of the earlier period has become rather plain and podgy and in general much less attractive. It was an issue which undoubtedly preoccupied him and which in the character of the ageing Rosita is expressed with great poignancy.

Even more central to Lorca's work as a whole is the theme of love and its attendant frustration. In *Blood Wedding* and *The House of Bernarda Alba* he had embodied love at its most passionate and physical in the characters of the Bride, Leonardo, and Adela. In the first, sexual frustration leads the Bride and her former lover, Leonardo, to run away on the day of her marriage to the Bridegroom, while, after the Bridegroom and Leonardo have killed each other in a knife-fight, the Bride is left to face the life-long frustration of widowhood. In *The House of Bernarda Alba*, such is Adela's despair when she is falsely informed that her lover has been killed that she commits suicide. In *Yerma*, completed after *Blood Wedding*, passion and frustration take a rather different form, for Yerma's desperate longing is for a child, her frustration the fact that she fails to produce one. Years earlier, in *Mariana Pineda*, Lorca had presented both themes in a rather different way. Mariana is deeply in love with Pedro de Sotomayor, the leader of the liberal group in Granada, and, when he leaves the country to escape arrest and probable execution, she lives with the hope that he will one day return, which he never does. Mariana's illusion and betrayal clearly anticipate in that respect the hopes which Rosita entertains for many years. In both plays, the presentation of love and frustration is less fierce and much more touching and poignant than in *Blood Wedding* and *The House of Bernarda Alba*, but the centrality of these themes in Lorca's work, whatever form they take, is deeply rooted in his personal experience. Whether or not he had a sexual relationship with Salvador Dalí in the late 1920s is very much a matter of conjecture, but there is no doubt that Lorca was strongly attracted to the painter. When Dalí became romantically involved with the woman known as Gala, whom he would later marry, it seems highly probable, therefore, that Lorca felt a strong sense of resentment. Furthermore, in 1928 Lorca had a homosexual relationship with a young Madrid sculptor, Emilio Aladrén Perojo, who a year later abandoned him for a young woman, Eleanor Dove, whom he married in 1931. If the themes of love, betrayal and frustration were present in Lorca's work before this, it is easy enough to understand the reason for their importance in the later plays.

Another of *Doña Rosita*'s major concerns, evident too in many other plays, is the damaging effect of gossip and public criticism. In the earlier *The Shoemaker's Wonderful Wife*, the Shoemaker and his much younger wife become the object of the villagers' cruel mockery because they have produced no children, a situation which is repeated in the later *Yerma*, in which Juan becomes increasingly concerned about the way in which, on account of their failure to have a child and Yerma's increasingly bizarre behaviour, they have become the object of local gossip. In Act Three, for example, he complains bitterly: 'And people are starting to talk . . . to talk openly. When they see me, they fall silent. And even at night in the fields, if I wake up, it seems as if the branches have suddenly gone quiet.' Similarly, in *The House of Bernarda Alba*, Bernarda's daughter Magdalena observes in Act One that in the past 'spiteful gossip wasn't the fashion' but that today 'we waste away for fear of what people might say'. In short, there is a readiness on the part of people to pick on and denigrate those who, not necessarily through any fault of their own, fall short of what is expected or regarded as normal, be it a failure to produce a child in marriage – an essential component of a Catholic marriage – or, indeed, a failure to marry, which is, of course, Rosita's fate. No less than the childless Yerma, she slowly becomes, therefore, the object of public ridicule, talked about by adults and openly mocked by their children, as she reveals in Act Three: 'But everyone knew the truth, and I'd find myself picked out by a pointing finger that made a mockery of my engagement [. . .] Girls and boys leave me behind because I can't keep up with them, and one of them says: "Look, there's the old maid." And another one, a good-looking boy with curly hair, says: "No one's going to fancy her." I have to listen to it all.'

In placing considerable emphasis on this essentially negative aspect of Spanish life, as common in cities like Granada as in rural communities, Lorca was, of course, channelling into dramatic form another part of his own experience. During his late teenage years, his attendance at the Café Alameda in Granada, the haunt of a group of intellectuals and creative artists which included homosexuals, had been a source of gossip. In adult life his relationships with Dalí, Aladrén and others could not fail to be noted, even though he often made great efforts to conceal his sexual inclinations. At the premiere of *Yerma* in 1934, abusive right-wing members of the audience had shouted 'Queer!', and he was also insultingly described by Ramón Ruiz Alonso, a right-wing ex-Member of Parliament for Granada as 'the poet with the fat head'. When he was finally murdered in August of 1936, Juan Luis Trecastro boasted that he had been one of the executioners and had put 'two bullets up his arse for being a queer'. Like many of the characters in his plays, but for a different reason, Lorca undoubtedly felt both persecuted and marginalised in a society which was intolerant of and unable to accept difference, and it is no surprise, therefore, that he should have made those feelings a central aspect of his work.

As well as this, *Doña Rosita* presents us with Lorca's view of the Granada bourgeoisie, which stems in turn from his socialist leanings. Given the fact that his father, Federico García Rodríguez, was a well-to-do landowner and that his background was, on that account, privileged, the young Lorca had nevertheless sympathised with the children in Fuente Vaqueros and Asquerosa who were far worse off than himself. It was a sympathy which was to colour the rest of his life; which led him, for example, to rage against the wealthy whites who exploited the poor blacks of New York; which made him an ally of the left-wing Republican Government, which came into power in Spain from 1931 to 1933, and again in February 1936; and which inspired various statements and actions during the last few years of his life, which proclaimed his support for the weak and the poor and his intense dislike of the kind of intolerance and complacency which he saw in the middle classes, not least in Granada. In this context, it is worth pointing out that the statement mentioned earlier in which he lamented the loss of a unique Muslim civilisation had been immediately followed by a withering attack on the present-day inhabitants of Granada whom he described as 'the worst middle class in Spain'. And even if the events of *Doña Rosita* are set in the past, as much as forty years before the actual composition of the play, there can be no doubt that Lorca's presentation of its middle-class characters also mirrored the Granada bourgeoisie of the 1930s. At the end of the nineteenth century – 1898 to be precise – Spain's once great empire, greater than that of any other European country in the sixteenth and early seventeenth centuries, had come to an end with the loss of Cuba and the Philippines, while internally Spain was racked by political, social and economic problems. In *Doña Rosita*, Lorca presents us with a middle class which turns its back on such problems, preferring to bury its head in the sand. The Uncle escapes into a world of flowers while his financial affairs become ever more disastrous. The Aunt spends her time embroidering and sewing, though it has to be said that these were activities to which at that time women were expected to restrict themselves. Most culpable of all are the Mother and her three daughters, all of them distinguished by an obsession with appearance and social climbing, which they endlessly pursue even though money is in short supply. In one respect their pretentiousness is highly comic, but it is also empty and as fragile as the flowers cultivated by the Uncle. Even though Mr X is, at the beginning of Act Two, an equally comic figure, his allusions to progress at the beginning of the twentieth century point to a world from which Granada's middle class, and by extension the Spanish middle class, is excluded. Instead, it spends its time gazing at its navel, locked into a world which is in reality falling about its ears. As for the Granada middle class of the 1930s, largely opposed to the left-wing progressive government of 1931–3, Lorca felt that little had changed.

The broader meaning: symbolism and imagery

In certain respects, *Doña Rosita* seems to be a naturalistic play, for it provides quite a detailed picture of Granada's bourgeoisie and there are frequent references in the text to real places, churches, dates, and families, while in each of its three acts costumes are described with an accuracy which pinpoints a particular time. Even so, throughout his career as a playwright, Lorca always rejected naturalism in favour of a dramatic technique which transformed the specific and local setting of a play into something much more universal. It would be surprising, therefore, if, in his penultimate full-length play, he would suddenly produce something that was entirely naturalistic, in complete contrast to the plays written just before it: *Blood Wedding* and *Yerma*.

In both these plays, the choice of generic as opposed to real names for most of the characters has the immediate effect of opening out the relevance of the action. To this extent, the Bride, the Bridegroom, the Mother, the Father, the Neighbour, the Servant of *Blood Wedding* become much more universal characters involved in events which could occur in countries other than Spain, and the same is true of Pagan Woman, First Woman, Second Woman, Male, Female in *Yerma*, including Yerma herself (the Barren One). For all its apparent realism, and despite its location in Granada, *Doña Rosita* employs the same technique, since the names are also for the most part generic: the Aunt, the Uncle, the Housekeeper, the Mother, the three Spinsters, Mr X, the Nephew, and even Rosita, although a real enough name and a diminutive of Rosa, has, through its association with the rose, a broader and more symbolic meaning.

Indeed, if the names of the characters serve to universalise the play's significance, Lorca's use of flower imagery throughout the text underpins that aspect of his dramatic technique. When, for example, Rosita makes her first appearance, she wears a 'rose-coloured dress', which at once emphasises beauty and the full flush of youth. But, more than this, her exit and her reappearance as she searches for her parasol frame the Uncle's description of the *rosa mutabilis*, whose colour in the morning is 'deepest red', by evening

'deadly pale', and, when night comes, devoid of petals. The
image of the rose which dies immediately evokes both Rosita's
present beauty and her ultimate fate as her hopes of marriage
to the Nephew fade with the passing years and she grows
older to the point at which, at the end of Act Three, she is
dressed in white, the equivalent of the dying rose.

Furthermore, the rose itself is more than just a symbol of
Rosita's fate. Rather, it is a perfect representation, as writers
have recognised throughout the ages, of the fragility and
vulnerability of both beauty and human happiness, and
Rosita, through her association with the rose, becomes an
image of all women who share her experience, as her words in
Act Three suggest: 'What's happened to me has happened to
thousands of others.' She might well have added: 'And will go
on happening.'

The play's flower symbolism is present too in other
characters, such as the three Manolas of Act One, and the
Mother and the three Spinsters in Act Two. Although the
Manolas are not, like Rosita, systematically linked to one
particular flower, the vivid colours of their dresses – 'The first
of them is dressed in green, / The second in deepest purple' –
similarly evoke the beauty and bloom of youth, while in
Rosita's description of them there are various allusions which
suggest both their association with the rose and with flowers
in general, be it with regard to their surroundings – 'Where do
the three girls go, / While the rose and the leaping fountain/
Suffer in deepest shadow?' – or their physical attributes –
'Whose hands will steal the perfume / From the flowers of
their breasts?' Furthermore, the Third Manola's suggestion
that 'Our bridal petticoats / Are edged with frost' not only
conjures up the image of a beautiful flower destroyed during
the night by heavy frost, but also links the Manolas to Rosita,
anticipating the way in which her hopes of love and marriage
to the Nephew will be doomed.

As for the Mother and the three Spinsters, the verses with
which they celebrate Rosita's birthday – 'What the Flowers
Say' – list a variety of flowers and their connection with the
different and contrasting emotions experienced in love: eternal
hope, trust, passion, bitterness, disdain, jealousy. The positive
aspect of love therefore alternates with its negative

counterpart, once more balancing hope and optimism with its opposite. Even so, of the young women who sing the song, only Rosita has experienced love, and even that will eventually fade. The three Spinsters and the two Ayola girls still look for love but may never find it, their fate perhaps suggested in the words of the Third Spinster: 'Dead flowers weep in your long hair, / Some are as sharp as knives'. Significantly, she appears again in Act Three, still unmarried. And finally, although at the end of Act Two the Uncle enters with the *rosa mutabilis*, whose blazing red colour here symbolises Rosita's beauty and the joy which the promise of marriage to her fiancé has just brought her, his observation that 'If I'd waited two hours more, it would have been white' has ominous implications. Throughout the play, then, Lorca's use of flower imagery is highly suggestive, both linking different characters and, beyond that, transforming their experiences of hope, love and disappointment into something which is much more universal and which applies to all those who seek and fail to find love.

Doña Rosita is also characterised by a number of enclosed spaces, all of which have a variety of symbolic implications. Foremost among these is, of course, the house. In Acts One and Two, the house, inhabited by Rosita, the Aunt, the Uncle, and the Housekeeper, and visited by others, is full of lively activity and conversation. In Act Three, following the Uncle's death, it is an empty place in which at night the Aunt can hear her cough echoing as if she were in church. The house therefore comes to symbolise at this point the emptiness of the Aunt's life and of Rosita's too, as she faces a future without much hope. Again, the house with its enclosed garden is in complete contrast to the open spaces of Argentina where, in the Aunt's words in Act One, the Nephew will be 'free to sail the seas and rivers, to ride through grapefruit groves'. He is, indeed, the only person in the family who escapes to a life of freedom, while Rosita and the Aunt are condemned to a life of unproductive domesticity and the Uncle to a self-imposed burden of accumulating debts. In this particular sense, the house with its enclosed garden can be seen as an image of Granada itself, which, cut off from the open sea by the Sierra Nevada and inhabited by a highly conservative and inward-

looking bourgeoisie, Lorca found stifling and claustrophobic.
The Albaicín, in which the house is set, was for him a
reminder of Granada's Moorish past, a place of magical
associations which he loved, but by the early twentieth
century it was also a place which was crumbling, and to that
extent representative both of Granada and a Spain in need of
transformation. Moreover, if the twisting, labyrinthine streets
of the Albaicín could be seen in one way as intriguing and
mysterious, they could also be seen, like Granada itself, as a
prison-like maze from which it was difficult to escape.

A second enclosed space which has a clear symbolic
meaning is the Uncle's greenhouse, from which he emerges at
the very beginning of the play and in which he spends a great
deal of time. Above all, the greenhouse embodies his
absorption and self-immolation in the world of flowers, to the
virtual exclusion of all else. As he admits in Act Two, he
prefers 'a bit of peace and quiet', escaping from domestic
affairs as much as possible in order to concentrate on his
flowers, and, although he loves Rosita dearly, it is very
noticeable that, unlike the Aunt and the Housekeeper, he
never becomes involved in the discussions about her
abandonment by the Nephew. Indeed, he drifts in and out of
the onstage action, returning on almost every occasion to the
cultivation of his flowers. The world they represent is,
moreover, an artificial one, and the flowers, despite their
impressive beauty, have a certain sterility, suggestive of the
enclosed, self-contained world in which the Uncle lives. In this
respect, it is significant that the Housekeeper should prefer
oranges, quinces, pears, plums, and cherries, in short, fruit
that is not cultivated artificially and that therefore belongs to
the vibrant world of Nature.

The enclosed and airless greenhouse is also, by extension,
symbolic of the self-absorbing concerns of many of the other
characters. The Mother and the three Spinsters are in this
sense like the Uncle, though concerned not with flowers but
with appearance, with making an impression, with keeping a
position in society, even at the expense of eating properly, as
the Mother indicates: 'Many's the time I say to them: "Tell
me, dear girls, which would you really prefer: an egg for lunch
or a seat at the evening promenade?" They all reply

immediately: "A seat, a seat!"' The two Ayola girls, daughters
of an extremely wealthy father, are concerned only with
finding a husband, and the Aunt and Rosita seem to spend
endless time sewing and embroidering clothes and sheets for
Rosita's bottom drawer. In other words, the activities of many
of the play's characters are very little different from those of
the Uncle, and Lorca suggests through them a way of life
which, typical of Granada's bourgeoisie and, indeed, of the
Spanish bourgeoisie as a whole, is ultimately stagnant and
inward-looking, far removed from the kind of progress which
would rescue the country from its inertia, and which is
eulogised by Mr X at the beginning of Act Two.

A third enclosed space, equally symbolic, is the school where
Don Martín is a teacher. In an ideal world, the school should
be a place of learning and enlightenment, attended by pupils
eager to learn from those employed to give them the benefit of
their knowledge. In reality, the school is for Don Martín and
his colleagues a place of imprisonment where they are at the
mercy of the children of well-to-do parents who care not a jot
for the welfare of the assistant teachers. Thus, Don Martín
and, to an even greater extent, Mr Canito and Mr Consuegra,
are the object of their pupils' bullying and cruel practical jokes,
which their parents, far from condemning, enjoy and approve
of: 'They pay, so we have to put up with them [the children].
The parents simply laugh at such pranks because we are only
assistants. I mean, we aren't the ones who mark the exams.
They think we have no feelings'. The point has been made
earlier that Lorca, himself the victim of bourgeois hostility and
intolerance, sympathised with the underprivileged and the
persecuted, and was highly critical of those who, because of
their wealth and social superiority, took advantage of those
whom they regarded as inferior. The behaviour of
inconsiderate children is portrayed, therefore, as a reflection of
bourgeois parents whose minds are closed to everything but
their own self-satisfied world, and the enclosed space of the
school can be seen as a further extension of the house and the
greenhouse, all suggestive of the inward-looking world which
Lorca often considered Granada to be.

In Lorca's plays in general, the tension created by opposites,
by the conflict of positive and negative forces, is very strong

indeed. In *Blood Wedding*, for example, the passion of the
Bride and Leonardo, which leads to their elopement, is in
direct conflict with her obligations to her new husband and
with society's demands that she respect her marriage vows.
In *Yerma*, the fecundity of Nature is seen to be in direct
opposition to Yerma's failure to produce a child. In both
plays, moreover, there is a network of images and allusions
which underpin those opposites and which, by setting the
action in a broader context, such as the context of the natural
world, extend its significance, investing it with a more
universal resonance. *Doña Rosita* differs from both *Blood
Wedding* and *Yerma* in the sense that the forces at work on
Rosita are less intense, and the outcome is much more sad
than tragic. Even so, as in the other two plays, there is a
tension of opposites, in this case of hope and disillusionment,
which is also enhanced by imagery. Rosita's hope for a bright
and happy future is, for example, embodied in the idealised
vision of her fiancé she presents to the three Manolas: 'Two
eyes / That make the darkness bright, / . . . Two eyes that,
though as black as jet, / Like poppies light the deepest night'.
When he promises her that he will return, he will do so in
'a ship of bright gold, its sails of pure joy', while Rosita
imagines that news of his return will be brought by 'a white
dove'. Even so, allusions which evoke future happiness are
soon combined with and outnumbered by others which
suggest the opposite. The Nephew's departure leaves Rosita
with 'A poisoned arrow straight through her heart'. She will
be left 'Like the strings of a lute struck dumb', and soon
wrapped in a 'shroud . . . made / From earth and water'. In
Act Three, when her hopes have finally been shattered, she
refers to the children watching the removal of furniture
'as if there were a corpse in the house'. As for her feelings, she
finds herself 'going round and round in a cold place', while,
despite her knowledge of what has happened, hope still
lingers, pursuing her 'like a dying wolf'. Images and allusions
which evoke light and happiness are therefore set against
others which suggest pain and suffering, the former uplifting,
the latter depressing. Their effect is to allow us to observe
in Rosita and to feel with her the joy and despair we have
all experienced at some time in our lives, and on that

account to see her unhappy lot as common to all humanity.

Important too in this respect is Lorca's use of the stage in terms of lighting, movement, costume, music, and poetry. Act One takes place in daylight, the lighting of the stage corresponding, at least at first, to Rosita's high spirits and, of course, her youth and beauty. In Act Two she is ten years older and her hopes of her fiancé's return are under strain, but the arrival of his letter and the party atmosphere associated with Rosita's saint's day again create a celebratory mood which is reflected in the lighting. By Act Three all has changed. A further ten years on, Rosita's hopes have disappeared, the now widowed Aunt is frail and unwell, and the move to a smaller house is under way. By the time they finally leave the old house, it is getting dark, '*The stage is in the half-light of evening*', the wind has risen, and the rain has started to fall. As in his other plays, Lorca suggests the increasing despondency of his characters through the growing darkness of the stage and thereby draws us, the audience, into identifying with their experience.

Movement in the play is also carefully orchestrated in order to suggest the progression from joy to despair. No sooner has the action begun than Rosita rushes in, the epitome of youthful high spirits, leaves quickly, then rushes in again in search of her parasol. Later in the act, her disappointed reaction to the news of her fiancé's departure is reflected in her lack of movement, firstly as they stand facing each other, and then as they sit. In Act Two, her agitation and sense of anticipation as she waits for the postman is reflected in her quick entrances and exits and her anxious pacing up and down. The arrival of the Mother, her three daughters and the two Ayola girls leads to the vigorous 'What the Flowers Say', during which the stage is full of activity, while the news contained in the letter provokes further high spirits and, at the end of the act, a joyous celebratory dance, reminiscent of the wedding reception in *Blood Wedding*, in which all the on-stage characters take part. Act Three, on the other hand, has a very different rhythm. The Aunt, ten years older and in a dejected mood, is initially seated in the now almost empty and lifeless house. When she gets up, she does so with difficulty, for, as the Housekeeper says, 'Your legs have gone stiff from too much sitting around'. Even the removal men move slowly, carrying a divan '*as if they are carrying a coffin*'. When Don Martín appears, his crippled leg means that he has to sit, and when he leaves, the Housekeeper has to help him out of his chair. When Rosita delivers her great speech – 'For many years I've grown accustomed to living outside myself . . .' – she does so from a kneeling position, and when she, the Aunt and the Housekeeper leave the house for the last time, Rosita almost faints and has to be supported by the two older women. In short, movement in the play corresponds to and underlines at every stage the emotional trajectory of the characters, functioning as visual signposts within the ebb and flow of their journey.

Closely allied to lighting and movement are colour and music. Colour is partly created, of course, by costume, and, as it is employed by Lorca, harmonises with his use of the other stage effects. In Act One, therefore, Rosita's rose-coloured dress is one with the brightness of an Andalusian day and the vigour of her movement, underlining the optimism of youth and hope for the future. Similarly, the green and purple of the Manolas' dresses, together on stage with the red of Rosita's, create a riot of colour. In Act Two her dress is more muted, red changing to pink in accordance with the mood of increasing doubt and fading hope. Because she is in mourning for her dead husband, the Mother wears dark colours, '*a faded black dress and a hat with old purple ribbons*', and, although Lorca does not specify colours for the exaggerated hats and dresses of the three daughters, they too would most likely be dressed in dark colours in memory of their father. Despite the high spirits of 'What the Flowers Say' and the dance at the end of the act, subdued colours therefore offset that sense of optimism, and these, of course, dominate the increasingly pessimistic mood of Act Three. After the death of her husband, the Aunt is dressed in black, matching in that respect the traditional dark clothing of the Housekeeper. And although it is not stated, Don Martín is also likely to wear a dark-coloured suit befitting his age and profession. Towards the end of the act, the Third Spinster appears in '*a dark dress with a mourning veil*'. As for Rosita, the colour of her dress has now become paler and, when she finally leaves the house, white, which points to a colourless and drab future. In this context, we should not forget, either, that the effects of differently coloured costume are accompanied throughout the play by the colours of flowers, both actual and linguistic. In Act One there are references to violets, roses, myrtle, jasmine, and many other flowers. In Act Two the Mother and her daughters speak of roses, violets, the syringa, while the song 'What the Flowers Say' evokes a wide range of beautiful flowers. And at the end of Act Two, the Uncle brings the dazzling *rosa mutabilis* on stage, its brilliant red underpinning the happy mood of that moment. In short, colour, like lighting and movement, is a key visual element in reinforcing mood and atmosphere as the action unfolds.

As a highly accomplished musician, Lorca was expert too at using music to enhance particular dramatic moments, whether with instrumental accompaniment, songs, or the rhythm of the language itself, especially in the form of poetry. In *The Shoemaker's Wonderful Wife*, for example, '*the sound of a flute accompanied by a guitar*' underpins the Wife's thoughts of imaginary suitors. In *The Love of Don Perlimplín*, piano music precedes the appearance of the beautiful, half-naked Belisa. In the second act of *Blood Wedding*, songs express the joy and enthusiasm of the approaching wedding guests, in Act Three two violins create the melancholy, menacing mood which surrounds the arrival of the three Woodcutters, synonymous with Fate, and throughout this and other plays Lorca introduces highly expressive poetic passages in order to pinpoint the drama and intensity of particular moments. *Doña Rosita* is yet another fine example of this technique, which also has the effect, of course, of broadening their relevance in the way that poetry and music always do.

Early on in Act One, the Uncle waxes lyrical about various kinds of roses and then reads from a book the lovely poem about the dazzling beauty and the rapid decline of the *rosa mutabilis*. It is an extremely moving piece, at this point without any clear reference to Rosita's future, even though her rose-coloured dress links her beauty to the rose. As the act unfolds, however, the connection between her and the fading rose grows steadily clearer, underlined by three linked and highly stylised poetic scenes. The first of these consists of her description of the three beautiful Manolas who vainly search for love. The second is the farewell scene between Rosita and her fiancé – its sad mood emphasised by a piano accompaniment – in which, despite his promise to return, her doubts and despair effectively make her a fourth Manola. And the third, in which she ends Act One by herself reading aloud the poem about the *rosa mutabilis*, confirms the relevance of the flower to her future. There is thus a progression through each of these scenes, their significance heightened by the manner in which, because they are in verse, they stand out like peaks in the surrounding landscape, not only allowing us to feel increasingly for Rosita as the truth becomes clear, but also to see her experience as true of other lovers and one to which we can ourselves relate.

In Act Two there is less poetry as such, but its introduction towards the end of the act is again highly effective. Before this, the verses of 'What the Flowers Say', with piano accompaniment, create a party mood appropriate to the celebration of Rosita's saint's day. But the lines spoken by Rosita in the course of the episode – 'The rose has opened quickly / In the early morning light' – seem to isolate her from the rest of the company, as though she has become obsessed with the *rosa mutabilis* and its relevance to herself. And although this is followed by the arrival of the Nephew's letter and a change for the better in Rosita's mood, the act ends with her once more referring to the final decline of the once beautiful flower, 'Like the whiteness of a dove, / Like the sea's sad smiling, / Like the pale white coldness / Of a cheek marked by grieving.' Here, then, there is a distinct contrast between the comic vibrancy of one kind of verse – the traditional verse of 'What the Flowers Say' – and the introspective, brooding nature of Rosita's lines, which has the effect of marking out the latter even more.

Act Three contains little poetry of a formal kind other than Don Martín's recitation of four lines from his unperformed and clearly badly-written play and Rosita's speaking of the final six lines of the poem about the rose, but it does have a number of prose passages which have both the rhythm and the heightened emotion of poetry: the Housekeeper's account of her anguish on the death of her husband and small daughter, and her distress at Rosita's current plight; her vision of herself, the Aunt, the Uncle and Rosita in heaven; and, above all, Rosita's immensely moving speech, 'For many years I've grown accustomed to living outside myself', as powerful and affecting as any verse.

Passages of a marked musical nature, on two occasions with musical accompaniment, occur, then, at key moments in the play, intensifying the mood in a way which draws us into the feelings expressed at that particular point. And in this context it is worth remembering that, when Lorca was in the process of writing his plays, he often listened to music in the form of gramophone records. It is not surprising, therefore, that the plays themselves should have acquired a strong musical character. Even so, as we have seen, this aspect of *Doña Rosita* should not be separated from all the other aspects of stage performance considered earlier. In integrating all the various elements of speech, song, lighting, costume and movement into a whole, Lorca followed the dramatic principles of theatre practitioners such as Maurice Maeterlinck, Adolphe Appia and Edward Gordon Craig, all of whom believed that a play should not, like photography, seek to capture a particular moment and a particular time in all its realistic detail, but, through the careful integration of all the different elements of stage performance, should seek to achieve an effect that was much more symbolic and universal.

The characters

Rosita

Lorca named only three of his plays after a female character: *Yerma*, *Doña Rosita* and *The Shoemaker's Wonderful Wife*. The title of *The House of Bernarda Alba* suggests, in contrast, the importance of the house and, by extension, those who form the household, even though Bernarda is the central character. As for Rosita, she is certainly one of Lorca's lovingly-drawn characters, and the play exposes her inner life and emotions in great detail in the course of its unfolding.

Initially, at twenty years of age, Rosita has all the vibrant enthusiasm of youth. When she first appears, she rushes in in search of her hat and, shortly afterwards, in search of her parasol. Like many young people, she is spontaneous, as much in her enthusiasms as in her disappointments, and if her early entrances and exits point to her exuberance and love of life, the news that her fiancé is returning to Argentina throws her into the depths of despair. The volatile and excited young woman becomes instead 'a lute struck dumb', convinced that her fiancé will not return and that her life is already over: 'My shroud shall be made from earth and water'.

By the beginning of Act Two ten years of waiting in vain have changed her, for now her eager grasping of the present moment has become an attempt to sustain an illusion which has little basis in reality. As the Housekeeper observes: 'I'd like to throw a shoe at her head at times. She stares into space so much, she'll soon have eyes like a cow's.' Aware that time is passing and her hopes of marriage fading, she now turns her back on the reality of her situation: 'I don't want to know that time is passing me by'. But even though we may regard Rosita as misguided and her clinging to hope as rather pathetic, we can also admire her steadfastness, her trust in her fiancé's promise to return, and the rejection of the advice of others that she should marry someone else: 'I wait for him now as I did on the very first day. Anyway, what's a year, or two years, or five?' When, shortly afterwards, the letter arrives in which he proposes marriage by proxy – an arrangement whereby someone stands in for him at the marriage ceremony – Rosita's delight is understandable, but the possibility that it is built on sand is exposed by the Housekeeper's down-to-earth query as to how, after this marriage by proxy, Rosita will spend her nights. By the end of Act Two, Rosita may be older and more mature, but she is also very clearly in denial.

After another ten years, as Act Three makes clear, denial has become the realisation that she has been abandoned for ever, for news has recently arrived of her fiancé's marriage in Argentina as long as eight years earlier, although she suggests that she knew of it long before this: 'I knew he'd got married. A well-meaning person insisted on telling me'. At all events, her long speech – 'For many years I've grown accustomed to living outside myself' – reveals her, in her acceptance of the situation, to be a woman of great dignity, resolved to endure her fate despite 'a mouth full of bitterness and a desperate longing to run away'. But even more moving is her admission that, although she knows that her hope of marriage to her former fiancé is no longer a reality, she still experiences it deep within herself: '. . . it pursues me, circles around me, gnaws at me; like a dying wolf trying to sink its teeth in for the last time.' And moving too is her resolve not to be defeated, even though she knows that she will eventually be alone, the Aunt and the Housekeeper no longer there to comfort her. In the course of the play, then, Rosita grows and develops as a human being, her initial exuberance and naivety transformed first into a clinging to fond but unsubstantiated illusion and finally into brave acceptance of her lot. In certain respects her development parallels that of Yerma in the play premiered a year earlier, although she is less desperate and ultimately less tragic.

The Aunt

Together with the Housekeeper, the Aunt is, after Rosita, the most fully developed and rounded character in the play. Having cared for Rosita since the death of her parents, the Aunt's devotion to her is unquestionable, and for that reason she is particularly upset by the Nephew's decision to return to Argentina, knowing full well how distraught Rosita will be. Nevertheless, the Aunt is also a woman of strong moral integrity, not only understanding that the Nephew has a duty to obey his father's request to return, but also because of that, urging him to fulfil that obligation in spite of the hurt to her niece: 'It's your duty to go. It's a big estate and your father's getting on. I have to make sure you get on the ship'. Furthermore, when the Housekeeper launches into several highly emotional verbal attacks on the Nephew, the Aunt often stops her in her tracks, revealing a self-control and sense of proportion which the servant lacks.

After the death of her husband, twenty years later, the Aunt is a much sadder figure, obliged to deal with his considerable debts and forced, on that account, to move to a smaller house. Her feelings for Rosita, now finally abandoned by her fiancé, are, though, as strong, if not stronger, than before: 'He should be made to pay with blood for what has cost us blood, even if it were all my blood'. And there is something immensely touching too in her comment, as she finally leaves the house, that, even though she will not be there, she will still be able to hear the greenhouse door banging in the wind – a beautiful touch on Lorca's part that reveals both the Aunt's connection with the house after so many years, and the place which her husband, custodian of the greenhouse for so long, still has in her heart.

Her relationship with him is also revealed to us in some detail. Her opening remarks in Act One – 'Hellebore, fuchsias and chrysanthemums, violet Louis-Passy, silver-white altair with heliotrope points' – suggest an irritation with his constant attention to his flowers and his evident expectation that everything else, including herself no doubt, take second place. When, after his death, it becomes clear that his obsession with his flowers, as well as his generosity to others, has resulted in considerable financial debts, her earlier irritation becomes, very naturally, a marked bitterness: 'The old fool! No head for business! Roses on the brain! No concept of money! He was ruining us day by day!'. Nevertheless, there is no doubt that her bond with him has been very close, for even as she criticises him, she adds that 'there was no misfortune he wouldn't try to put right, no child he wouldn't try to help [. . .] because he was so kind hearted [. . .] the purest Christian soul!' In the course of the play, they frequently cross swords, but, as he perceptively observes in Act Two, arguments between two people who have been together for many years, are often their way of trying to keep boredom at bay. In short, the relationship between the Aunt and the Uncle is extremely true to life and brilliantly observed. And the same is true of her relationship with the Housekeeper. Throughout the play they have differences of opinion, but because they have been together for many years, they know each other's strengths and weaknesses. At one point they argue to the point where the Housekeeper is dismissed, but almost immediately they are as one again.

The Uncle

The key to the Uncle's character lies in his comment to the Aunt in Act Two: 'What's the point of discussing it? I prefer a bit of peace and quiet – make my bed, wash my suits, rearrange the rugs in my room.' Although he is close to his wife, he likes his independence and has come over the years to prefer his own company, no doubt because he is surrounded by women – his wife, Rosita and the Housekeeper – and clearly has no sons. His greenhouse is therefore a means of escape, and, although he is very fond of Rosita, he is fonder still of his flowers, lavishing on them enormous care and affection. In contrast to the Aunt, the Uncle appears on stage on only a few occasions, and when he does so his conversation is usually connected to his plants, sufficient indication of the central place they occupy in his life. His dedication to this activity, combined with the carelessness with which he administers his financial affairs and which eventually incurs his debts, suggests that he is not a practical person, or that, if he once was, he has turned his back on the world, losing himself in horticulture.

The Housekeeper

The Housekeeper is one of Lorca's most brilliantly portrayed servants, anticipating and certainly rivalling Poncia in *The House of Bernarda Alba*. In contrast to the people for whom she works, she lacks formal education, but this is more than compensated for by a typical working-class practicality. When, for example, it is suggested in Act Two that the Nephew will marry Rosita 'by proxy', her ridicule of such a fanciful idea is typical of her down-to-earth approach to life: 'What about the nights? [. . .] The bedsheets and covers trembling with cold.' The comment is also one which points to an unsentimental appreciation of the physical pleasures of life exemplified in her preference for the taste of fruit over the scent of flowers, and in a directness which, as her remarks early in Act One suggest, is the very opposite of the Aunt's sophistication: 'Our mouths are made for eating, / Our legs are made for dancing, / But then there is a woman's thing, / And that is made for . . .' On the other hand, although she is extremely practical, her lack of education means that she is also highly superstitious, frequently uttering spells which she hopes will do harm to the young man who has abandoned her beloved Rosita.

While the people who employ her have had a relatively comfortable life, the Housekeeper's has at times been very difficult, typical in that respect of her class. In Act Three, for example, she speaks of her grief at the death of her husband and her daughter: 'When I buried my little girl – you'll know what I mean – when I buried my little girl, it was just as if they were stamping on my insides.' And in Act One she refers to the poverty her family has endured: 'And my own children, shivering with hunger in a wretched hovel!' In this context, it is understandable that she has no patience either with those who have airs and graces or those who have great wealth. In Act Two her comment on the arrival of the Mother and her spinster daughters – 'All show and just stale crumbs to keep them going' – is later followed by her sarcastic comment on the two Ayola girls – 'The esteemed daughters of the high and mighty Ayola, photographer to His Majesty the King'. And in Act Three she launches into a vitriolic attack on the recently deceased Don Rafael Salé, exploiter of the poor: 'He's on his way to hell, of course! He'll be pleading with them [the demons]: "I've got twenty million pesetas, don't touch me with those tongs! Forty thousand duros to take those burning coals away from my feet!" But it won't stop those demons. A prod here, a poke there, a kick elsewhere. They'll smack his face till his blood turns to charcoal!'

Despite all this, the Housekeeper's relationship with the Uncle, the Aunt and Rosita is very close, based on the many years she has worked for the family. She clearly adores Rosita and is committed to her happiness. When the young woman is abandoned by the Nephew, she is therefore just as upset, if not more so, as the Aunt, cursing him throughout the play for his callousness and his final treachery. Her love for Rosita is revealed too in the gift of the ornate thermometer which she proposes to give her on her saint's day. As for her relationship with the Aunt, it is one in which, more like a family member than a servant, she does not hesitate to speak her mind, even though her frankness often gets her into trouble. In Act Two, for example, her refusal to hold her tongue leads to her dismissal from her position, but in no time at all she is back in the Aunt's good books and the Aunt in hers. In spite of their social differences, the Housekeeper and the Aunt are, indeed, inseparable companions. In short, the Housekeeper is, perhaps, the most vividly drawn and detailed character in the play, and she is certainly a source of much greater humour than Poncia in *The House of Bernarda Alba*.

The other characters

Of the characters outside the Aunt and Uncle's household, the schoolteacher Don Martín, and the Professor of Social Economy, Mr X, are portrayed in the greatest detail, both markedly different from each other. Don Martín is both comic and rather pathetic, a dignified man with an air of considerable sadness. The incongruity between the fact that he is old and lame yet dyes his hair in order to appear younger strikes a comic note, and this is reinforced by the evident gulf between his ambition to be a writer and the lack of talent demonstrated by the terrible lines from his play, *Jephthah's Daughter*, which, unsurprisingly, has failed to reach the stage, and whose atrocious quality he cannot recognise: 'Oh, mother unequalled! Turn your eyes on her / Who lies before you in wretched trance! / Receive unto yourself these shining jewels! / Observe the fatal horror of death's advance!' There is, on the other hand, a good deal of pathos in the reality of his day-to-day circumstances. The fact that he is a bachelor links him to the lonely spinster characters of the play, but his plight is worse than theirs, for he has no one to look after him and seems incapable of looking after himself properly, as the Housekeeper suggests in Act Three: 'When he was ill, I took him some custard. The bedsheets were as black as coal, and as for the walls and the wash-basin . . . You've never seen the like!' As well as this, Don Martín is merely an assistant teacher at the school where he is employed, poorly paid on that account, and also abused, as we have seen, by both the pupils and their well-to-do parents. Nevertheless, there is in Don Martín a certain stoicism and acceptance of his situation which invite a degree of admiration: 'We must do our best

through acts of kindness and sacrifice.' Far from being a one-
dimensional character, then, Don Martín personifies the
mixture of the comic and the sad, laughter and tears, which
run throughout the play.

Mr X, in contrast, is entirely one-dimensional, a pompous,
ridiculous and overbearing individual lacking any trace of
humility. In his long conversation with the Uncle at the
beginning of Act Two, his attitude is one of condescension: 'A
professor of Political Economy shouldn't really be talking to a
rose-grower.' He brushes aside the Uncle's observations,
thrusts his own opinions on the importance of science and
progress down his throat, and clearly loves naming the
important people with whom he claims to be acquainted: 'the
Shah of Persia – a quite delightful fellow'; 'I knew [Marcel]
Renol well'. In short, Mr X is a comic exaggeration of whom
Lorca makes fun, his saint's-day present to Rosita as
overblown as he is himself: 'a mother-of-pearl Eiffel Tower
over two doves who bear in their beaks the wheel of industry'.
His attempt to win Rosita's affection is entirely laughable and
his failure to do so wholly deserved.

The Nephew, already engaged to Rosita before the action of
the play begins, appears in person, and rather briefly, only in
Act One. Although he has been in Granada for sufficient time
to win Rosita's hand, his reason for being there is otherwise
unexplained. He is described by the Aunt as someone who has
spent his time 'admiring the flowers', which suggests that he is
somewhat idle. As well as this, he seems to be rather spineless,
for he initially tries to avoid telling Rosita that he is returning
to Argentina and asks the Aunt to give her the news on his
behalf: 'I'll be back in a minute. Perhaps you'll tell her.' It is
uncertain whether the following farewell scene is real or
imagined, given its marked stylisation, but, imagined or not,
the Nephew's assurances of love and his promise to return
smack of a desire to appease her more than anything else.
Although this is the last we see of him, he is still a constant
presence in Acts Two and Three, for his letters to Rosita
sustain her hopes of their marriage in the future. But his
insincerity is finally revealed by the fact that he continues to
write to her in the same vein even after he has married
someone else. The Aunt's suspicions about him in Act One are

certainly justified by the end of the play. He is an individual
who is entirely unworthy of Rosita's love.

The three Manolas are friends of Rosita who live in Elvira
Street, in 1890 the main thoroughfare of Granada. They are
clearly acceptable to Rosita's family and, by implication,
thoroughly respectable, though, as Rosita's poetic account of
them in Act One suggests, their visits alone to the Alhambra
are the subject of common gossip, which portrays them as
rather dubious young women. Lorca makes little distinction
between them, for they are one in their beauty, in their search
for love, and in their failure, at least in Act One, to find it. To
a certain extent, they are therefore symbolic of Granada's
spinsters, their experience sad and depressing, and a pointer to
what Rosita's future will eventually be. Later on, in Act
Three, however, we meet the son of the eldest Manola, now
dead, who informs the Aunt that his mother's sister lives in
Barcelona and has four children. In other words, two of the
Manolas of Act One subsequently found the love which they
initially sought. Coming at this point, as Rosita acknowledges
that her hopes of marriage have disappeared, the information
has the effect of emphasising the pathos of her situation.

The Mother and the Three Spinsters are the comic
equivalent of the Manolas, distinguished in this case not by
their beauty but by their exaggerated clothing: '*The three*
SPINSTERS *wear enormous hats with tasteless feathers, absurd
dresses, elbow-length gloves with bracelets over them, and
fans dangling from long chains. The* MOTHER *wears a faded
black dress and a hat with old purple ribbons.*' In appearance
they are reminiscent of some of the characters in Lorca's
farces and puppet plays – Don Blackbird, for example, in *The
Shoemaker's Wonderful Wife* – lacking any kind of subtlety
not only in the way they dress, but also in the way they speak.
When the Mother makes her entrance in Act Two, her
greeting to Rosita, far from being a simple 'Happy saint's
day', is an overblown 'Felicitations!', and the way in which
her three daughters, chorus-like, repeat the word, suggests
that they are mere replicas of the Mother. She, however, has
the most to say and is by far the most developed character,
though almost her entire conversation revolves around dress,
social standing, and the sacrifices she has been obliged to

make in order to keep up appearances. But even though Lorca satirises and to that extent condemns her misplaced pretentiousness, he also sympathises with the three spinsters, as he did with many other women who were desperate to marry but who were left on the shelf in a society which mocked them.

The two Ayola girls, unlike the Spinsters, have a rich father, photographer to the king of Spain. When we first see them in Act Two, they are therefore '*expensively dressed*', but they are also rather empty-headed, laughing uncontrollably at the slightest thing and thinking only of attending weddings and finding someone to marry as quickly as possible. Furthermore, they are spiteful creatures, as the First Ayola's comment to the Spinsters suggests: 'Girls without one [a boyfriend] are faded dried-up creatures, all of them . . . (*Glancing at the* SPINSTERS.) well, some at least . . . boiling up inside.' In the Spinsters, Lorca satirised social pretentiousness, in the Ayola girls, the condescension of the rich to those less fortunate than themselves.

The eighteen-year-old Youth who appears towards the end of Act Three, son of the eldest Manola, is briefly portrayed but, as the Aunt observes, has a good sense of humour, denigrating his own looks in favour of his mother's: 'Mine were put together with a hammer'. His sense of fun is revealed in his account of how, at carnival time, he put on his now dead mother's dress, but his sensitivity is also evident in the fact that, when his resemblance to her reduces his aunt to tears, he weeps too. And there is also all the gaucheness of adolescence in his embarrassment when the Housekeeper teases him about his girlfriend. In short, the Youth seems to be a thoroughly pleasant individual, but his main function in the play, appearing when he does, is clearly to suggest to us all what Rosita might have had, thereby intensifying her sense of loss.

The comic element

The comic tradition in Spanish theatre is, of course, old and well-established. In the fifteenth century, the stock comic

characters and the stylised situations of the Italian *commedia
dell'arte* were to be found in the plays of Gil Vicente, Juan del
Encina and Torres Naharro. In the sixteenth and seventeenth
centuries, the short comic pieces of Lope de Rueda and
Miguel de Cervantes were full of boldly-drawn characters,
amusing situations, and down-to-earth language. It was a
tradition which, in the late nineteenth and early twentieth
century, influenced as important a dramatist as Ramón del
Valle-Inclán, several of whose plays employ the techniques of
farce and contain puppet characters, in some cases to satirise
Spanish society, in others to comment on the human
condition. The latter was also the concern of Jacinto Grau,
who, in *Mr Pygmalion*, portrayed the creator of a number of
life-size puppets who subsequently becomes a puppet in their
control. The tradition of puppet play and farce was one with
which Lorca was completely familiar and one which therefore
influenced his own work to a considerable degree.

There are, in fact, very few if any Lorca plays in which
there is no comic element. Furthermore, the range of comedy
is extremely wide, embracing very broad comic effects on the
one hand, and much more subtle comic moments on the
other. The puppet plays and farces fall into the first of these
two categories, as in the case of *The Puppet Play of Don
Cristóbal*, subtitled *A Farce for Puppets*. This short piece is
characterised by bold, uninhibited emotions, embodied in the
sexually insatiable Rosita and the bullying and lecherous Don
Cristóbal, as well as by the violent nature of his actions. At
the end of the play, for example, Rosita suddenly gives birth
to five children, who Don Cristóbal suspects are not his, and
in a moment of rage he kills her mother, who, seconds later,
comes back to life. Similarly, in *The Shoemaker's Wonderful
Wife*, subtitled *A Violent Farce*, the clashes between husband
and wife are physically and linguistically aggressive and highly
comic, while other characters, such as Don Blackbird '*dressed
in black, a long-tailed coat and short trousers*', are amusing
caricatures. Even so, this is a play in which these broad comic
strokes are balanced by Lorca's evident compassion for the
Shoemaker and his wife, who are constantly hounded by the
gossip and the mockery of the other villagers. The mixture of
the comic and the serious is even more to the fore in *The Love*

of Don Perlimplín, for the ridiculous spectacle of Perlimplín in the marriage bed, cuckolded during the night by his new wife's five lovers and therefore '*with two golden horns on his head*', is offset by compassion for the deluded old man, not least when, having disguised himself and convinced his wife that he is her handsome but anonymous young lover, he commits suicide.

In the major plays, comic elements are, of course, more subtle, based on the interplay of characters and what they say rather than what they do. In *Blood Wedding*, a highly intense and dramatic play, a lighter comic note is struck, for example, by the response of the naive and rather gauche Bridegroom when he takes his leave of his bride-to-be: 'When I leave your side I feel a great emptiness and a kind of lump in my throat.' In *Yerma*, another extremely powerful drama, there is a typically comic element in Act One, Scene Two, when the Second Girl speaks of her mother's resolve to ensure her daughter's pregnancy: 'And next October we have to go and pray to the Saint [. . .] My mother'll be doing the praying, not me.' And in the increasingly dark and tragic *The House of Bernarda Alba*, there are also amusing moments, such as Magdalena's comment on the physical appearance of Angustias: 'If she looked like a stick wrapped in a dress at twenty, what's she like now at forty?' But if there are comic moments to be found even in the tragedies, no Lorca play combines the comic and the serious as consistently and as brilliantly as *Doña Rosita*.

The broadest comedy is to be found in the exaggerated appearance of the Mother and the Three Spinsters, their '*enormous hats with tasteless feathers, absurd dresses*', etc., reminiscent of caricatured characters in the puppet plays and farces. But if the comic element is in part visual, it lies too in the nature of their conversation, which is invariably pretentious and, of course, at odds with the reality of the financially straitened circumstances in which they live. In the light of this, the Mother's remarks are, for us, if not for her, highly amusing: 'What agonies I've gone through, madam, so my girls should not be deprived of hats! The tears I've shed on account of a ribbon or an arrangement of curls!' Yet, as we have seen, Lorca undoubtedly felt a degree of sympathy for the spinster status of the three girls, and the comic nature of their appearance and of their Mother's absurd objectives are balanced by a certain pathos.

Pretentiousness is also a source of amusement in the case of Mr X, the Professor of Social Economy, though here without the slightest element of sympathy. In contrast to the Mother and her daughters, there is no indication of what Mr X looks like or of how he is dressed, but, like them, he is essentially a one-dimensional character about whom we learn nothing other than the fact that he is full of bombast, given to name-dropping, and totally uninterested in the opinions of other people. On the other hand, Don Martín is, as we have already seen, a much more complex and rounded individual, and the comic element is therefore much more subtle and varied. As much as any other character, he invites the mixture of laughter and tears which is so characteristic of this play and at which Lorca shows himself to be such a master.

Otherwise, comic moments in the play frequently arise from the interplay of two or more characters, especially the Aunt and the Housekeeper. A perfect example of this occurs in Act Two, when the Aunt objects to the Housekeeper's outspokenness and an argument develops between them as to which of them loves Rosita most. Undoubtedly, the exchanges between the refined mistress and the outspoken servant – like table-tennis in their rapidity – are highly amusing, not least because the two women are so fond of each other, but more amusing still is the way in which, when the Housekeeper has been sacked, they are not only quickly reconciled, but the spectacle of the Housekeeper's present for Rosita leads the Aunt to admit that the Housekeeper loves Rosita more than anyone, which she has earlier denied, and which the Housekeeper now refuses to accept. It is an episode full of superbly arranged changes of position, and totally character-based.

There are many other examples of this in the course of the play. The Aunt is, for example, often obliged to rein in the spells and curses which the highly superstitious Housekeeper launches in the direction of Rosita's feckless fiancé, or to try to cut short her garrulousness. Similarly, there are comic moments involving exchanges between the Housekeeper and the Uncle in relation to his flowers. But Lorca's triumph in this play is also to interweave these moments of comedy with Rosita's increasingly desperate situation. In Act One, light-hearted exchanges between the Aunt and the Housekeeper give way to the dramatic scene in which the Nephew reveals to the Aunt his decision to return to Argentina. This, in turn, is followed by the comic moment in which the Housekeeper, having overheard their conversation, curses the Nephew, and this by the highly poetic episode involving Rosita and the three Manolas and the extremely stylised farewell scene between Rosita and the Nephew. As in a piece of music, the light-hearted and the solemn are interwoven with great skill.

The second act follows the same pattern, although the comic episodes are in fact more frequent. The highly amusing opening scene between the Uncle and Mr X is followed almost straight away by the argument between the Aunt and the Housekeeper over which of them loves Rosita most. Following this, the conversation between the Aunt and the Uncle is rather strained, and this develops into an even more serious episode in which Rosita dismisses the Aunt's advice that she should marry someone other than the Nephew and insists that, in spite of passing time, her love for him is the same as it ever was. But the appearance of the Mother and her daughters and, just afterwards, the two Ayola girls, begins an extended comic situation which lasts almost until the end of the act, when laughter and celebration are finally offset by a moment of doubt associated with the *rosa mutabilis* and its transformation from red to deathly white.

Act Three, focusing on the Aunt's loneliness after the death of her husband, her bitterness on account of the debts he has left her, her anger over the Nephew's betrayal of Rosita, and Rosita's abandonment of any hope of marriage, has a much more serious character, but even so this is at times interwoven with brilliantly comic moments. The highlight in this respect is, of course, the arrival of Don Martín, which moves the emphasis of the play away from the Aunt's and Rosita's predicament to the more amusing matter of his literary aspirations and the tricks played on the teachers by their pupils. But even when he has left, the comic note is sustained in the Housekeeper's account of how the wealthy and

exploitative Don Rafael Salé will be tortured in hell and of
how she, the Aunt, the Uncle, and Rosita can look forward to
a good time together in heaven, 'in an armchair of sky-blue
silk, rocking, cooling ourselves with fans of scarlet satin'. The
appearance of the Youth later on and his account of how he
put on his mother's dress introduces another light-hearted
note, but then the predominantly serious tone of this act is re-
established as Rosita, the Aunt, and the Housekeeper abandon
the old house for ever. Much more than in any other of his
plays, Lorca achieves in *Doña Rosita* a seamless and sustained
mixture of laughter and tears.

For this very reason, a comparison has often been made
between Lorca and Chekhov, in particular between *Doña
Rosita* and *The Cherry Orchard*. Both plays focus on a family
in decline and on a home which, for financial reasons, has to
be sold. In Chekhov's play, as well as in much of his other
work, there is that bitter-sweet quality which distinguishes
Doña Rosita, as well as caricatured characters through whom
Chekhov satirises a particular society. As for Lorca's
knowledge of Chekhov, Francisco García Lorca has noted
that he and Federico were familiar with Chekhov's short
stories when they were teenagers in Granada. It is clear too
that the Russian dramatist was much admired by the theatre
director, Cipriano Rivas Cherif, a friend of Lorca who also
directed several of his plays, and who formed an experimental
theatre company, El Caracol, in 1929, which performed
Chekhov's work. And in 1932 a Russian company performed
The Cherry Orchard at the Teatro Español in Madrid, which
Lorca, in all probability, would have seen. But even if Lorca
had some knowledge of Chekhov's work and its frequently
bitter-sweet character, it is equally true that the mixture of the
comic and the serious coloured Lorca's plays from the
beginning and was undoubtedly an integral part of his own
personality.

Staging of Lorca's plays in his lifetime

The production of Lorca's first play, *The Butterfly's Evil
Spell,* which opened at the Teatro Eslava in Madrid on 22

March 1920, was an unmitigated disaster. The original intention of the theatre impresario, Gregorio Martínez Sierra, was that the play should be performed by puppets, which might well have been more effective, but in the end it was presented by actors, the role of the Butterfly performed by the leading ballet dancer, Encarnación López Júlvez, 'La Argentinita'. The set and costumes were extremely colourful and the music used at particular points in the play was by Grieg. From the outset a section of the audience, clearly hostile to any kind of experimentation in the theatre, seemed determined to ruin the evening, and the reviews which appeared in the following morning's newspapers were not much more encouraging.

Although Lorca worked on a number of puppet plays and farces between 1922 and 1927, his second production was *Mariana Pineda,* which he had completed in 1924, and which was premiered at the Teatro Goya in Barcelona on 24 June 1927, the eponymous heroine played by the famous actress Margarita Xirgu, who would become increasingly involved in Lorca's work, and the sets designed by Salvador Dalí. Although the play was performed only six times in Barcelona, for Margarita Xirgu's company ended their season there on 28 June, it was warmly received by the critics, as it was when the production opened in the following autumn at the Teatro Fontalba in Madrid. Contemporary reviews of the Madrid production emphasise both the highly poetic nature of Lorca's treatment of the historical subject, so familiar to Spaniards, and the stylisation of the production in which sets and costumes played such an important part. M. Fernández Almagro, the theatre critic of the newspaper, *La Voz,* spoke of the exquisite simplicity of Dalí's designs, a view echoed by E. Díez-Canedo in *El Sol.* In short, despite the fact that *Mariana Pineda* was a historical play and therefore open to a naturalistic treatment, Lorca's poetic approach to it, underlined by the production itself, points to the general thrust of his theatre as a whole.

It was again Margarita Xirgu who played the lead part in the premiere of *The Shoemaker's Wonderful Wife* at the Teatro Español in Madrid on 24 December 1930. Particularly interesting about this production was the fact that Lorca himself, dressed in a star-spangled cloak, read the prologue in which the Author appears on stage and informs the audience of the need for poetry and magic on the contemporary stage. In its staging, the play evidently put into practice Lorca's intentions, for the sets and costumes, based on drawings by the dramatist himself, and influenced by Picasso's designs for Manuel de Falla's *The Three-Cornered Hat,* matched the character of the play in their bold, vibrant colours and combined perfectly with vigorous movement and language to recreate on the modern stage all the vitality of a long puppet play tradition. Lorca's piece ran for some thirty performances and greatly strengthened his working relationship with Margarita Xirgu.

The spring of 1933 saw two triumphant premieres which increased Lorca's fame as a playwright: *Blood Wedding* at the Teatro Beatriz in Madrid on 8 March, and *The Love of Don Perlimplín for Belisa in his Garden* on 5 April at the Teatro Español, both directed by Lorca himself. Lorca's work was now being influenced greatly by his own experience as a director with the touring company, 'La Barraca', which provided him with an ever deepening knowledge of the practicalities of performance. The reviews of *The Love of Don Perlimplín* point to the colourful stylisation of the production, enhanced by the music of Scarlatti. At the end of May 1933 the Madrid production of *Blood Wedding* opened in Barcelona, and in July another production of the play was a great success in Buenos Aires before going on tour and returning to the city in October. It ran for several months, made Lorca a good deal of money and established his reputation in Argentina. In December, moreover, the same company opened with *The Shoemaker's Wonderful Wife,* which proved to be equally successful.

Lola Membrives, whose company produced both plays in Buenos Aires, was anxious to stage another play of Lorca's in early 1934, and, in the absence of a new work, decided to present *Mariana Pineda,* which opened on 12 January. In spite of the fact that the famous actress took the part of Mariana, this early play of Lorca's was compared unfavourably with *Blood Wedding* and the production was not a great success. In contrast, *Yerma,* the second play in his rural trilogy, was a

complete triumph when it opened on 29 December at the
Teatro Español in Madrid, with Margarita Xirgu in the title
role. Initially, right-wing extremists, enraged by Lorca's
homosexuality and left-wing sympathies, as well as by
Margarita Xirgu's support for Manuel Azaña, a leading left-
wing politician who had recently been imprisoned, attempted
to disrupt the performance, but they were then thrown out of
the theatre. When the curtain fell, the reaction of the audience
was rapturous, and Lorca himself was obliged to make
numerous appearances on stage.

1935 saw a number of important productions of Lorca's
plays in Spain. While *Yerma* continued at the Teatro Español,
the company of Lola Membrives had returned from Buenos
Aires and on 28 February opened at the Madrid Coliseum
with her production of *Blood Wedding*. Less than a month
later the company, giving two performances each evening as
was the Spanish practice, gave *Blood Wedding* at the first
performance and *The Shoemaker's Wonderful Wife* at the
second. In the first quarter of 1935 Lorca therefore had three
plays running in Madrid, an unheard-of event in the theatre of
that time. By the middle of the year he had also finished
writing *Doña Rosita the Spinster,* which Margarita Xirgu
proposed to include in her forthcoming season in Barcelona.
The season of one month at the Teatro Barcelona opened on
10 September with a production of Lorca's adaptation of
Lope de Vega's *The Foolish Lady,* followed a week later by
Yerma, the success of which was as great as it had been in
Madrid. On 5 November the company performed *Yerma* at
the Teatro Principal in Valencia, the second production in a
short season there, and then returned to Barcelona where
Margarita Xirgu would present both *Blood Wedding* and
Doña Rosita the Spinster at the Principal Palace Theatre. The
former opened on 22 November to great acclaim, the sets
designed by José Caballero and the music directed by Lorca
who also accompanied on the piano the lullaby in the second
scene of Act One. If anything, the premiere of *Doña Rosita
the Spinster* on 12 December was an even greater success.
Writing in *La Vanguardia,* María Luz Morales commented in
particular on the way in which the play induced laughter and
tears at the same time, and on how, through both prose and

poetry, the mood of Granada through a quarter of a century is so delicately and evocatively created by the writer. In Barcelona Lorca's play was performed to packed houses, regular articles about him appeared in the newspapers, a special performance of the play was put on for the flower-sellers of the Ramblas, and, at the end of the year there was a magnificent banquet at the Majestic Inglaterra Hotel, attended by Catalonia's artists and intellectuals. Lorca was indeed at the height of his fame.

In January 1936 Margarita Xirgu left Spain for Cuba, where, on 16 February she presented *Yerma* in Havana to enthusiastic audiences. On 18 April she opened her season in Mexico with the same play and subsequently presented *Doña Rosita the Spinster, The Shoemaker's Wonderful Wife* and *Blood Wedding*. In Spain itself there were to be no productions, although Lorca was at work, as always, on a variety of projects. The work which has been discussed above, as well as the plays he was now either writing or planning, provide abundant evidence of the extent to which he was always eager to experiment and seek new forms of theatrical expression. But what is even more surprising is the fact that such an innovative dramatist should also have triumphed in the commercial theatre of his day.

Production history of *Doña Rosita the Spinster*

The premiere
The account of the *rosa mutabilis*, read to Lorca by his friend José Moreno Villa in 1924, was, as we have seen, the inspiration for the story of Doña Rosita. Over the next ten years it gradually took shape in his imagination, as was the case with many of his other plays. Dulce María Loynaz, the daughter of a wealthy Cuban family, has recalled, for example, that, during his stay in Cuba in 1930, Lorca accompanied at the piano some of the verses that appear in Act One of the play. In late December of 1934 he stated in a newspaper interview that he was working on a new play, *Doña Rosita the Spinster*, 'a comedy of middle-class manners', and in a slightly later interview amplified that statement by

describing the play as dramatising 'the tragic aspect of our social life: all those Spanish women who never found a husband'. By the early summer of 1935 he had completed it, and in July read it to Margarita Xirgu, her husband Miguel Ortín, and the theatre director Cipriano Rivas Cherif, now the director of Xirgu's company. In September she took the leading role in *Yerma* in Barcelona, and in November returned to the city's Principal Palace Theatre to play the role of the Mother in *Blood Wedding* and that of the main character in *Doña Rosita the Spinster*.

The premiere of *Doña Rosita* took place on 12 December 1935, directed by Rivas Cherif and designed by Manuel Fontanals. Along with Margarita Xirgu, they had been responsible for the production of *Yerma* in Madrid one year earlier and were therefore totally familiar with the style of production of which Lorca approved. Furthermore, Lorca was heavily involved in the performance of his new play, for he and Xirgu spent many hours discussing aspects of its staging, and he was himself, as an accomplished musician, responsible for the music.

The opening night was an unqualified triumph, the theatre critics unanimous in their praise. Reviewing the play for the Madrid newspaper *El Sol*, Antonio Espina concluded that 'the tone of this work is rather different from that which has distinguished the stage-plays of García Lorca up to this point. But it is, nevertheless, typical Lorca. For its antecedents one has to look back to *Mariana Pineda* [. . .] The dramatic colouring of *Doña Rosita* intensifies gradually as the action unfolds. The final act is an extremely difficult and challenging balancing act which speaks volumes for the skill of this dramatist. He has succeeded in making this play one of the very best in modern theatre, both in Spain and beyond.' And this affirmation of Lorca's place in the theatrical world was echoed by María Luz Morales in the Barcelona newspaper *La Vanguardia*: 'this play affirms, without any question, his [Lorca's] vocation and direction as a dramatist [. . .] It is a play of very fine literary qualities, but its essence – I repeat – is theatrical. It can be favourably compared with the best productions in European theatre today.'

More specifically, Antonio Espina drew attention in Act

One to the pure lyricism of the episode involving the Manolas and the 'sober yet exquisite tenderness' of the farewell between Rosita and the Nephew, concluding that it provided 'ample scope for the poet to move with complete freedom in that lyrical atmosphere which is his natural medium when it comes to expressing oneself'. As for Act Three, he regarded it as 'magisterial. Those noble women, Doña Rosita, the Aunt and the Housekeeper, emerging from the house, overwhelmed by a fate which has not allowed them to escape from the pain of financial ruin, which deprives them even of the roof which in other times protected the family's good fortune, form a proud elegiac triptych.' María Luz Morales saw the second act as 'chillingly grotesque' and as one of Lorca's great achievements: 'Everything in this act is completely admirable [. . .] The author [. . .] conceals his tenderness in irony, but he is never harsh with his characters: he pities them at every moment; he smiles indulgently in the face of their deficiencies, and in his smile there is deep pain.' As for Act Three, she considered it, like Antonio Espina, to be the best of all, the part of the play which 'provides the greatest challenge to the dramatist, and which leaves one with the strongest and most lasting impression'.

Rather surprisingly, in the light of Lorca's preference for stylisation in all aspects of his plays, the sets designed by Manuel Fontanals seem to have contained a much greater element of naturalism than those for the earlier production of *Yerma*. A photograph of the set for Act One, for example, shows Rosita and the three Manolas in the sitting room of the house against a background composed of a large window flanked by heavy curtains. To either side of the window, the walls are decorated with striped wallpaper and there are also paintings of landscapes and portraits. The room is furnished too with tables and velvet-backed chairs. In a second photograph, with Rosita, the Mother and the spinster daughters of Act Two, the design, in particular the background, is rather more spare – the scene is set ten years later – though realistic tables and chairs are still a prominent feature. The two critics mentioned earlier had little to say about the sets, although María Luz Morales considered it 'unfair not to mention the sets of Fontanals'. In general, they were thought to reflect the different periods in which the three acts take place.

The costumes evidently followed Lorca's suggestions very closely, for in her review Luz Morales noted that in Act One 'Rosita is an opening bud, displaying the most dazzling red, as do the Manolas'. Neither reviewer refers specifically to the colour of the costumes in Acts Two and Three, but a photograph of Rosita with the Mother and the Spinsters shows her to be wearing a dress much lighter in colour than that of Act One, and it seems safe to assume that the pink indicated by Lorca would have been adopted here, as well as white at the end of the play. The point is reinforced by the fact that María Luz Morales in particular drew attention to the 'ridiculous dresses' of the Mother and her daughters, at one with Lorca's original stage direction.

The performance of Margarita Xirgu in the title role attracted unqualified praise. Antonio Espina considered that the actress realised to the full 'the way the protagonist's feelings changed in the course of the journey marked by the three different periods', and that she displayed consummate skill in gesture, movement and delivery of her lines. María Luz Morales was impressed by the way in which Xirgu 'lived the three periods of *Doña Rosita* with exquisite intelligence and sensibility'. In a subsequent study of Xirgu's life and art, Antonina Rodrigo has drawn attention to the actress's ability to use her hands expressively, and the photographs of the production clearly underline this point. Of her portrayal of Rosita in general, Antonio Espina noted that 'The character of Doña Rosita has become an unsurpassable, unforgettable creation [. . .] in the career of our wonderful actress. Those present rewarded Margarita Xirgu with repeated curtain-calls.' The rest of the company also received praise, not so much individually but as an ensemble. Lorca, given his experience with his own theatre company, La Barraca, would have thoroughly approved.

Later productions
Lorca's murder by fascist supporters in the summer of 1936 meant that his plays were not performed again in Spain until

the early 1960s, when the iron grip of the Franco dictatorship began to ease somewhat. But it is surprising to note that, for whatever reason, *Doña Rosita* did not have a second major staging until 1980, forty-five years after the first production. On this occasion it was produced by the Centro Dramático Nacional, the Spanish National Theatre based in Madrid, and the role of Rosita was played by Nuria Espert, an actress as famous in recent times as Margarita Xirgu had been in the earlier period. The play was directed by the Argentinian theatre director, Jorge Lavelli.

While the sets for the Barcelona production of 1935 were marked by a degree of naturalism, photographs of this second production reveal much more stylisation. Designed by Max Bignens, all three acts took place in a single room, the appearance of which changed as the play unfolded. The features of the room were suggested simply and boldly. Upstage were two large wardrobes with mirrored doors, one on either side of the stage and at a slight angle. Across the back of the stage, at regular intervals, were three wooden frames which had the appearance of doorways, and behind which were rows of shelves on which flowerpots could be placed. Greenery suspended from above emphasised the greenhouse-like atmosphere, but otherwise, with the exception of one or two chairs, the stage was totally bare. The same set was employed in both Acts One and Two, but when, in Act Three, the family prepares to move house and the furniture and flowerpots have been removed, the frames and shelves suggested not so much a lived-in room but the skeleton of a room whose bones have been picked bare. In this respect, the set became an extremely evocative image, but its austerity also had the effect of allowing the attention to fall firmly on the acting area and therefore on the performance of the actors.

With regard to the costumes, Rosita appeared in Act One not in the dazzling red of the Barcelona production, but in a rose-pink dress, which by Act Three had, of course, faded to white. Furthermore, the dresses of the Manolas in Act One were not the same colour as Rosita's, as in the original, but much darker, which served to highlight Rosita's youth and optimism. As for the Mother and her daughters in Act Two, they were, as Lorca suggested, provided with large feathered hats and extravagant full-length dresses with flounces and tassels, all black in colour, reminiscent of great birds. In contrast, the lively but superficial Ayola girls wore white blouses and trousers, with boaters on their heads, suggesting both their youthful high spirits and, given their father's wealth, their wish to be modern and fashionable. In Act Three, the Aunt, Don Martín and the Housekeeper were all dressed in black, emphasising the play's darkening mood, and when Rosita finally left the house, she appeared in a long coat which revealed a dress as white as the dying rose. Furthermore, she dragged behind her the now useless wedding-dress, a sad pointer to her empty future.

In the summer of 1983 this production was presented with great success at the Edinburgh International Festival. Robert Cushman in the *Observer* noted of the set that it was 'used to frame a production' in the manner of a picture-frame, while B. A. Young in the *Financial Times* and Michael Billington in the *Guardian* commented on the effectiveness of the costumes. Most attention, however, was focused on Nuria Espert's performance as Rosita. In the *Sunday Telegraph*, Francis King drew attention to the emphasis placed by the actress on physical movement, contrasting Act One in which 'she radiates youth and hope dancing around the wide bare stage' with Act Three, in which she becomes 'a huddled ghost stalking the room, her mirror telling her that it is too late'. It was a view echoed by John Barber in the *Daily Mail*: 'The sense of a wasted life is conveyed by a slight crouch, huddled arms, and a habit of walking heavily, as if caged in, around the walls of the room.' Furthermore, Mary Brennan concluded in the *Glasgow Herald* that physical movement was, in Espert's performance, always the expression of something deeper, for 'she has the ability to make every external action seem a spontaneous expression of an inner state'.

Although a great deal of attention was given by the critics to Espert's performance, the acting of the other members of the company was also highly praised. John Barber considered that 'the actress-manager is supported by her troupe of eighteen, directed by Jorge Lavelli with tender care'. And Mary Brennan felt that the varying moods of the play were 'brilliantly conveyed by Julia Martínez, Carmen Bernardos,

Carla Lucena and Joaquín Mola'. But the last word should,
perhaps, be left to Michael Billington, who expressed the hope
that 'Edinburgh audiences won't [. . .] leave it to the last
minute to discover they have a miracle in their midst'.

The first British production of *Doña Rosita* was staged, in
this translation, at the Theatre Royal, Bristol (the Bristol Old
Vic), in October 1989, directed by Phyllida Lloyd. As in the
Espert production, there was a single set, designed by
Anthony Ward. It evoked a conservatory with a sloping glass
roof, covered by white cotton blinds and filled with flowerpots, thereby suggesting not only the Uncle's greenhouse but
the extent to which his obsession with plants and flowers
spilled over into the house itself. In addition, the enclosed
setting drew attention to the stifling, claustrophobic nature of
Rosita's existence. Towards the end of Act Three, moreover,
the blinds were opened to reveal storm clouds scudding across
the sky, a visual image of Rosita's sense of desolation, as well
as a visual pointer to the turmoil in the life of the family. As
for Rosita's costumes, they generally followed Lorca's
suggestions – red in Act One, pink in Act Two, white in Act
Three. In contrast, the costumes and hats for the Mother and
the three spinster daughters were certainly more exaggerated
than either Lorca's indications or their realisation in the Xirgu
and Espert productions. Indeed, the hats appeared to have the
most extraordinary shrubs growing out of them; for Nicholas
de Jongh in the *Guardian* they were reminiscent of birds
'which look as though they would be shot in the countryside'
and were 'on the verge of the preposterous'. This element of
exaggeration was further emphasised when, as Act Two drew
to a close, the Mother suddenly produced a trombone from
behind a shrub and produced several raucous and out-of-tune
notes on it. There is no justification for it in the text, and the
effect, combined with the ridiculous hats, was undoubtedly to
reduce these sad and lonely characters to sheer caricatures,
and to deprive them of the compassion which, even though he
disapproved of their pretentiousness, Lorca felt for them.

The acting, on the other hand, attracted considerable praise.
Jeremy Brien in *The Stage* noted that 'Susan Curnow brings a
captivating radiance and dignity to the title role', and Michael
Schmidt in the *Daily Telegraph* suggested that she 'brings

Rosita to her stark maturity with conviction. There is nothing
pathetic about her: she despises the pity she occasions.' As for
the other major roles, Nicholas de Jongh observed that 'Eve
Pearce's Aunt vividly, poignantly ages inexorably in a
performance of fine lines and sharp signs of decrepitude',
while Kate Kellaway in the *Observer* described it as 'first
class'. Jeremy Brien also praised the highly effective episodes
involving the Aunt and the Housekeeper: 'It is the interplay of
Eve Pearce, as her [Rosita's] benevolent aunt, and Sandra Voe,
as the warm-hearted and outspoken housekeeper, that brings
the most delightful and moving moments of a strong
relationship to the surface.' But the actors playing the lesser
parts – the Uncle, Mr X, Don Martín, for example – were also
praised for their performances.

In 1997 Phyllida Lloyd revived the play in a different
translation at the Almeida Theatre, London, but the reviews
on this occasion were more mixed. Several theatre critics,
including Benedict Nightingale in *The Times*, considered that
the production was too English: 'The final impression is of an
honourable English stab at a tricky play, but maybe too
honourable. And certainly too English.' In this context, it has
to be said that in English productions of Lorca's plays, actors
often perform from the neck up, lacking the passion and the
physicality which a Spanish actor would bring to a role, and
that directors, lacking knowledge of the Spanish background,
fail to realise the dramatist's intentions.

Another production, in my own translation, was staged at
the Jean Cocteau Repertory Theatre in New York in 2003–4.
Many of the reviews revealed a complete unfamiliarity with
the play, but in many respects they proved to be quite
positive. D. J. R. Bruckner, in the *New York Times*, for
example, found a 'stylistic gulf between the first two acts [. . .]
and the last', but concluded that this production overcame the
difficulty. Considerable praise was afforded to Amanda Jones
in the role of Rosita. A reviewer (unnamed) on the web
observed that 'As the title character [. . .] she does indeed
bring great sweetness and depth to Doña Rosita's sad odyssey
from hopeful youth to hopeless middle age. Our hearts break
as we see a vivid young woman, fresh as one of her uncle's
beloved roses, condemn herself to an arid life in a changing

but still rigid society through her misplaced loyalty to a
feckless fiancé.' The same critic commented favourably too on
some of the other performances: 'The sizeable ensemble is
headed by Cocteau regulars Elise Stone and Craig Smith, who
acquit themselves well as the aunt and uncle; Eileen Glenn
who wrings every ounce of humour from the role of the
meddling housekeeper; Michael Surabian who does double
duty as the amusing Mr X and Don Martín, the schoolteacher
whose life of regrets is something of a male counterpart to
that of Doña Rosita.' Little was said about the sets other than
that they were 'distinctly Spanish', or indeed the costumes, but
D. J. R. Bruckner concluded that the two hours of playing
time revealed much about the playwright and constituted 'a
generous gift'. Quite clearly, critical reaction to the few
productions which have taken place suggests that this is a play
which should be staged much more often.

Translating Lorca

In order to produce a successful English translation of a Lorca
play, it is essential to have a good knowledge of both Spanish
and the background in which the action of the play is set. The
background of *Doña Rosita* is rather different from that of
Blood Wedding, Yerma, and *The House of Bernarda Alba* in
the sense that it portrays not a peasant or rural community
but middle-class Granada society, which means that the
characters are generally more sophisticated and therefore
speak a language which is more refined than that of the rural
plays. Furthermore, the topics of conversation are very
different. The rural plays are full of allusions to and images
from the world of nature. In *Blood Wedding* the Mother uses
images of a bull and a carnation when speaking of her dead
husband, and in *Yerma* the eponymous heroine compares her
lack of fertility to a desert which only produces weeds. In
contrast, the allusions to flowers in *Doña Rosita* are not to
those that grow in the fields but to those cultivated by the
Uncle in his greenhouse. As for the other characters, they
discuss not the condition of the land or the prices of horses
and sheep, but the matters one associates with well-to-do

people who live in towns and are better educated. In one sense it is easier to transpose into English topics with which we are more familiar, but in another the fact that *Doña Rosita* is set as far back as 1890 means that problems often arise with regard to issues relating specifically to that period.

The one character in the play who does not belong to Granada's well-to-do society is, of course, the Housekeeper, an uneducated, working-class woman who, like Poncia in *The House of Bernarda Alba*, speaks in the down-to-earth, colloquial language of her class. She frequently resorts to proverbs, a common trait among such people, or casts spells on the Nephew which are difficult to translate because they contain allusions which make no sense. The contrast between the language she employs and that of the people for whom she works is considerable, but it forms a vital part of the linguistic richness and the comic impact of the play. It has to be conveyed by the translator and, of course, convincingly performed by the actress who plays the role.

The biggest problem for the translator of *Doña Rosita* is presented, however, by the passages in verse. It is essential, for example, to convey the lyricism and beauty of the poem about the *rosa mutabilis* in Act One, but in this respect the Spanish pattern of assonance, whereby the last syllable of alternate lines has the same stressed syllable – here, for example, 'quem*a*r', 'cor*a*l', relumbr*a*r' – and creates an easily formed rhyming pattern, cannot be achieved in English. In order to capture the flow and aesthetic effect of the verse, it is therefore preferable to employ rhyme:

> The stars advance across the sky,
> The wind no longer calls,
> And on the edge of darkness
> Her petals start to fall.

The same argument largely applies to 'What the Flowers Say' in Act Two, but opting for rhyme also involves sometimes rearranging the syntax of the Spanish line or even the order of some lines, though the meaning should remain the same.

The most difficult passage of all to translate is undoubtedly the Act One farewell between Rosita and the Nephew. It is impossible to be dogmatic on this point, but the dialogue here might not be taking place in reality but, rather, imagined by the three Manolas as the Housekeeper takes them aside to inform them of what is happening. At all events, the language of the original play is tremendously heightened, which fits in with the Manolas' romantic nature and their constant preoccupation with searching for love. To translate the dialogue as it stands seems too sentimental, certainly for a modern audience, and could well provoke laughter, which would in turn destroy the desired effect of the episode. In a previous translation – see note on p. 108 – I translated the passage much as it was in Spanish. I have now toned it down somewhat, though it still remains the most extreme poetic passage in the play.

Further Reading

Plays by Lorca in English translation

Lorca Plays: One (*Blood Wedding* [*Bodas de sangre*] and
  Doña Rosita the Spinster [*Doña Rosita la soltera*], trans.
  Gwynne Edwards, and *Yerma*, trans. Peter Luke), London,
  Methuen Drama, 1987
Lorca Plays: Two (*The Shoemaker's Wonderful Wife* [*La
  zapatera prodigiosa*], *The Love of Don Perlimplín* [*Amor
  de Don Perlimplín*], *The Puppet Play of Don Cristóbal*
  [*El retablillo de Don Cristóbal*], *The Butterfly's Evil Spell*
  [*El maleficio de la mariposa*], and *When Five Years Pass*
  [*Así que pasen cinco años*], trans. Gwynne Edwards),
  London, Methuen Drama, 1990
Lorca Plays: Three (*Mariana Pineda* and *Play without a Title*
  [*Comedia sin título*], trans. Gwynne Edwards, and *The
  Public* [*El público*], trans. Henry Livings), London,
  Methuen Drama, 1994
Blood Wedding, trans. Gwynne Edwards, with commentary
  and notes, London, Methuen Drama, 1997
The House of Bernarda Alba/La casa de Bernarda Alba, trans.
  Gwynne Edwards, English/Spanish text with commentary
  and notes, London, Methuen Drama, 1998
Yerma, trans. Gwynne Edwards, English/Spanish text with
  commentary and notes, London, Methuen Drama, 2007

Full-length studies of Lorca

Adams, Mildred, *García Lorca: Playwright and Poet,* New
  York, George Braziller, 1977. An informative biography
  based on personal reminiscence.
Allen, Rupert C., *Psyche and Symbol in the Theatre of
  Federico García Lorca,* Austin and London, University of
  Texas Press, 1974. Contains a section on the psychology of
  Yerma.

Anderson, Reed, *Federico García Lorca,* London, Macmillan, 1984. A useful study of Lorca's theatre as a whole.

Binding, Paul, *Lorca: The Gay Imagination,* London, Gay Men's Press, 1985. An examination of Lorca's work from a gay perspective.

Byrd, Suzanne, *'La Barraca' and the Spanish National Theatre,* New York, Ediciones Abra, 1975. A useful examination of Lorca's work as a director with his travelling theatre company.

Cano, José Luis, *García Lorca: Biografía ilustrada,* Barcelona, Destino, 1962. As well as an account of Lorca's life, this book contains many interesting photographs of Lorca, his family, friends and professional colleagues.

Correa, Gustavo, *La poesía mítica de Federico García Lorca,* Madrid, Editorial Gredos, 1975, 2nd ed. A detailed study of the role of myth and nature in Lorca's work as a whole.

Doggart, Sebastian, and Michael Thompson, *Fire, Blood and the Alphabet: One Hundred Years of Lorca,* Durham, University of Durham, 1999. A collection of essays on different aspects of Lorca's work.

Durán, Manuel (ed.), *Lorca: A Collection of Critical Essays,* New Jersey, Prentice Hall, 1962. Contains twelve essays on Lorca's poetry and theatre by academics and creative writers.

Edwards, Gwynne, *Lorca: The Theatre Beneath the Sand,* London, Marion Boyars, 1980. A comprehensive study of Lorca's theatre which includes sections on staging.

Edwards, Gwynne, *Dramatists in Perspective: Spanish Theatre in the Twentieth Century,* Cardiff, University of Wales Press, 1985. Chapter 3 examines Lorca in the context of European theatre.

Edwards, Gwynne, *Lorca: Living in the Theatre,* London, Peter Owen, 2003. Discusses the way in which Lorca's personal dilemmas are transformed into high art in his major plays.

García Lorca, Francisco, *In the Green Room: Memories of Federico,* trans. Christopher Maurer, London, Peter Owen, 1989. A translation of *Federico y su mundo,* Madrid, Alianza Editorial, 1980. Contains reminiscences of theatre productions as well as analyses of plays.

Gibson, Ian, *Federico García Lorca: A Life*, London, Faber and Faber, 1989. An authoritative biography.

Higginbotham, Virginia, *The Comic Spirit of Federico García Lorca*, Austin, University of Texas Press, 1976. Concentrates on Lorca's theatre within the context of puppet plays and farces.

Honig, Edwin, *García Lorca*, New York, New Directions, 1963. A general introduction to Lorca's work.

Lima, Robert, *The Theater of García Lorca*, New York, Las Americas Publishing Co., 1963. A detailed study with particular emphasis on fate.

Martínez Nadal, Rafael, *Lorca's 'The Public': A Study of his Unfinished Play (El Público) and of Love and Death in the Work of Federico García Lorca*, London, Calder and Boyars, 1974. A wide-ranging and dense study of Lorca's work as a whole, in particular of his most difficult play, *The Public*.

Morla Lynch, Carlos, *En España con Federico García Lorca: Páginas de un diario íntimo, 1928–36*, Madrid, Aguilar, 1958. Contains personal reminiscences and interesting background material to Lorca's work.

Piasecki, Andy, *File on Lorca*, London, Methuen Drama, 1991. One of the Methuen Writer-Files series. Contains synopses of Lorca's plays, as well as observations taken from various sources, including reviews of productions.

Smoot, Jean J., *A Comparison of Plays by John Millington Synge and Federico García Lorca: The Poets and Time*, Madrid, Ediciones José Porrúa Turanzas, 1978. Studies in particular the parallels between Lorca's three rural tragedies and some of the plays of Synge.

Stainton, Leslie, *Lorca: A Dream of Life*, London, Bloomsbury, 1998. A detailed and lively account of Lorca's life.

Warner, Robin (ed.), *Yerma*, Manchester, Manchester University Press, 1994. A critical edition of the Spanish text with introduction and notes.

Shorter studies of *Doña Rosita*

Cifuentes, Luis Fernández, 'Doña Rosita la soltera o El
lenguaje de las flores', *Cuadernos Hispanoamericanos*,
433–4 (1986), pp. 317–40.

Devoto, Daniel, '*Doña Rosita la soltera*: estructura y fuentes',
Bulletin Hispanique, 69 (1967), pp. 407–40.

Doménech, Ricardo, 'Nueva indagación en *Doña Rosita la
soltera*', *Anales de la Literatura Española Contemporánea*,
11 (1986), pp. 79–90.

Greenfield, Sumner, '*Doña Rosita la soltera* y la poetización
del tiempo', *Cuadernos Hispanoamericanos*, 433–4 (1986),
pp. 311–16.

Jiménez-Vera, Arturo, 'The Rose Symbolism and the Social
Message in *Doña Rosita la soltera*, *García Lorca Review*, 6
(1978), pp. 127–38.

Nickel, Catherine, 'The Function of Language in García
Lorca's *Doña Rosita la soltera*', *Hispania*, 66 (1983), pp.
522–31.

Recuerda, José Martín, *Análisis de 'Doña Rosita la soltera o
El lenguaje de las flores'*, Salamanca: Universidad, 1979.

Rodrigo, Antonina, 'En torno a *Doña Rosita la soltera*', in
García Lorca en Cataluña, Barcelona: Planeta, 1975, pp.
371–418.

While the majority of the shorter studies are in Spanish, non-Spanish speakers should note that there are chapters or sections on *Doña Rosita* in many of the full-length studies of Lorca listed earlier, notably in those by Reed Anderson, Gwynne Edwards, Francisco García Lorca, Virginia Higginbotham, and Robert Lima.

Doña Rosita the Spinster

or

The Language of the Flowers

A Poem of Granada in 1900,
Divided into Various Gardens,
With Scenes of Song and Dance

Doña Rosita la Soltera

o

El lenguaje de las flores

El lenguaje de las flores
Poema granadino del novecientos,
dividido en varios jardines,
con escenas de canto y baile

translated by Gwynne Edwards

PERSONAJES

DOÑA ROSITA

EL AMA

LA TÍA

MANOLA 1a

MANOLA 2a

MANOLA 3a

SOLTERA 1a

SOLTERA 2a

SOLTERA 3a

LA MADRE DE LAS SOLTERAS

AYOLA 1a

AYOLA 2a

EL TÍO

EL SOBRINO

EL CATEDRÁTICO DE ECONOMÍA POLÍTICA

DON MARTÍN

EL MUCHACHO

DOS OBREROS

UNA VOZ

CHARACTERS

DOÑA ROSITA
THE HOUSEKEEPER
THE AUNT
FIRST MANOLA
SECOND MANOLA
THIRD MANOLA
FIRST SPINSTER
SECOND SPINSTER
THIRD SPINSTER
MOTHER OF THE SPINSTERS
FIRST AYOLA
SECOND AYOLA
THE UNCLE
THE NEPHEW
THE PROFESSOR OF POLITICAL ECONOMY
DON MARTÍN
THE YOUTH
TWO WORKMEN
VOICE

Acto primero

Habitación con salida a un invernadero.

TÍO. ¿Y mis semillas?

AMA. Ahí estaban.

TÍO. Pues no están.

TÍA. Eléboro, fucsias y los crisantemos, Luis Passy violáceo y altair blanco plata con puntas heliotropo.

TÍO. Es necesario que cuidéis las flores.

AMA. Si lo dice por mí . . .

TÍA. Calla. No repliques.

TÍO. Lo digo por todos. Ayer me encontré las semillas de dalias pisoteadas por el suelo. (*Entra en el invernadero.*) No os dais cuenta de mi invernadero; desde el ochocientos siete, en que la condesa de Wandes obtuvo la *rosa muscosa* no la ha conseguido nadie en Granada más que yo, ni el botánico de la Universidad. Es preciso que tengáis más respeto por mis plantas.

AMA. Pero ¿no las respeto?

TÍA. ¡Chist! Sois a cuál peor.

AMA. Sí, señora. Pero yo no digo que de tanto regar las flores y tanta agua por todas partes van a salir sapos en el sofá.

TÍA. Luego bien te gusta olerlas.

AMA. No, señora. A mí las flores me huelen a niño muerto, o a profesión de monja, o a altar de iglesia. A cosas tristes. Donde esté una naranja o un buen membrillo, que se quiten las rosas del mundo. Pero aquí . . . rosas por la derecha, albahaca por la izquierda, anémonas, salvias, petunias y esas flores de ahora, de moda, los crisantemos, despeinados como unas cabezas de gitanillas. ¡Qué ganas tengo de ver plantados en este jardín un peral, un cerezo, un caqui!

TÍA. ¡Para comértelos!

AMA. Come quien tiene boca . . . Como decían en mi pueblo:

La boca sirve para comer,
las piernas sirven para la danza,
y hay una cosa de la mujer . . .

Act One

A room leading to a greenhouse.

UNCLE. Where on earth are my seeds?

HOUSEKEEPER. They were there.

UNCLE. Well, they aren't there now.

AUNT. Hellebore, fuchsias and chrysanthemums, violet Louis-Passy, silver-white altair with heliotrope points . . .

UNCLE. One has to be careful with flowers!

HOUSEKEEPER. I hope you don't mean that I . . .

AUNT. Be quiet! Don't answer back!

UNCLE. I mean everyone. Why, only yesterday I found the dahlia seeds trampled to bits. (*He goes into the greenhouse.*) You've no idea what this greenhouse means. In 1807 the Countess of Wandes produced the musk rose. Since then no one in Granada has managed it, except me. Not even the botanist at the university. So please have more respect for my plants.

HOUSEKEEPER. Do you mean I don't respect them?

AUNT. Ssh! You are the worst of all!

HOUSEKEEPER. No doubt, señora. But it's not me that says that with all this spraying and watering we'll soon have toads jumping out of the sofa!

AUNT. You know how you like to sniff at the flowers.

HOUSEKEEPER. Not me, señora. As far as I'm concerned, flowers smell of a dead child, or a nun, or the altar in a church. Sad things, all of them. Just give me an orange or a juicy quince, and you can keep your roses! But here it's roses to the right, basil to the left, anemones, sage, petunias, and these newfangled chrysanthemums with heads as scruffy as gypsy-girls! If only the garden had pears, or plums, or cherries!

AUNT. So you could eat them?

HOUSEKEEPER. What else is a mouth for, señora? There was a saying in my village:

Our mouths are made for eating,
Our legs are made for dancing,
But then there is a woman's thing,
And that is made for . . .

Se detiene y se acerca a la TÍA *y lo dice bajo.*

TÍA. ¡Jesús! (*Signando.*)

AMA. Son indecencias de los pueblos. (*Signando.*)

ROSITA (*entra rápida. Viene vestida de rosa con un traje del novecientos, mangas de jamón y adornos de cintas*). ¿Y mi sombrero? ¿Dónde está mi sombrero? ¡Ya han dado las treinta campanadas en San Luis!

AMA. Yo lo dejé en la mesa.

ROSITA. Pues no está. (*Buscan.*)

El AMA *sale.*

TÍA. ¿Has mirado en el armario?

Sale la TÍA.

AMA (*entra*). No lo encuentro.

ROSITA. ¿Será posible que no se sepa dónde está mi sombrero?

AMA. Ponte el azul con margaritas.

ROSITA. Estás loca.

AMA. Más loca estás tú.

TÍA (*vuelve a entrar*). ¡Vamos, aquí está!

ROSITA *lo coge y sale corriendo.*

AMA. Es que todo lo quiere volando. Hoy ya quisiera que fuese pasado mañana. Se echa a volar y se nos pierde de las manos. Cuando chiquita tenía que contarle todos los días el cuento de cuando ella fuera vieja: «Mi Rosita ya tiene ochenta años» . . . y siempre así. ¿Cuándo la ha visto usted sentada a hacer encaje de lanzadera o frivolité, o puntas de festón o sacar hilos para adornarse una chapona?

TÍA. Nunca.

AMA. Siempre del coro al caño y del caño al coro; del coro al caño y del caño al coro.

TÍA. ¡A ver si te equivocas!

AMA. Si me equivocara, no oiría usted ninguna palabra nueva.

TÍA. Claro es que nunca me ha gustado contradecirla, porque ¿quién apena a una criatura que no tiene padres?

She pauses, goes over to the AUNT, *whispers in her ear.*

AUNT (*crossing herself*). Heavens above!

HOUSEKEEPER (*crossing herself*). That's village life for you, señora!

> ROSITA *rushes in, wearing a rose-coloured dress in the style of 1900, with leg-of-mutton sleeves and trimmed with braid.*

ROSITA. My hat! Where's my hat? The bells of San Luis have rung thirty times already!

HOUSEKEEPER. I left it on the table.

ROSITA. Well, it's not there now.

They hunt for the hat. The HOUSEKEEPER *exits.*

AUNT. Have you looked in the wardrobe?

The AUNT *exits.*

HOUSEKEEPER (*entering*). I can't find it.

ROSITA. Doesn't anyone know where my hat is?

HOUSEKEEPER. Wear the blue one with the daisies.

ROSITA. Are you completely mad?

HOUSEKEEPER. Not half as mad as you are.

AUNT (*entering again*). Here it is!

> ROSITA *grabs the hat and rushes out.*

HOUSEKEEPER. Rush, rush, rush. Everything at top speed. She'd prefer today to be the day after tomorrow. She's off like a shot, here one minute, gone the next. Even when she was small I had to tell her a story about her being an old woman: 'Rosita at eighty' we called it. Tell me, when have you seen her sitting quietly, doing some lace-work, embroidering a cap?

AUNT. Never.

HOUSEKEEPER. She's always from shout to sheet and sheet to shout, shout to sheet and sheet to shout.

AUNT. You take care you don't say something you don't intend.

HOUSEKEEPER. If I do, señora, it won't be something you haven't heard before.

AUNT. Of course, I've never liked to say 'no' to her. Who wants to upset a child without a proper mother and father?

AMA. Ni padre, ni madre, ni perrito que le ladre, pero tiene un tío y una tía que valen un tesoro. (*La abraza.*)

TÍO (*dentro*). ¡Esto ya es demasiado!

TÍA. ¡María Santísima!

TÍO. Bien está que se pisen las semillas, pero no es tolerable que esté con las hojitas tronchadas la planta de rosal que más quiero. Mucho más que la muscosa y la híspida y la pomponiana y la damascena y que la eglantina de la reina Isabel. (*A la* TÍA.) Entra, entra y la verás.

TÍA. ¿Se ha roto?

TÍO. No, no le ha pasado gran cosa, pero pudo haberle pasado.

AMA. ¡Acabáramos!

TÍO. Yo me pregunto: ¿quién volcó la maceta?

AMA. A mí no me mire usted.

TÍO. ¿He sido yo?

AMA. ¿Y no hay gatos y no hay perros, y no hay un golpe de aire que entra por la ventana?

TÍA. Anda, barre el invernadero.

AMA. Está visto que en esta casa no la dejan hablar a una.

TÍO (*entra*). Es una rosa que nunca has visto; una sorpresa que te tengo preparada. Porque es increíble la *rosa declinata* de capullos caídos y la *inermis* que no tiene espinas; ¡qué maravilla!, ¿eh?, ¡ni una espina!; y la *mirtifolia* que viene de Bélgica, y la *sulfurata,* que brilla en la oscuridad. Pero ésta las aventaja a todas en rareza. Los botánicos la llaman *rosa mutabile,* que quiere decir mudable, que cambia . . . En este libro está su descripción y su pintura; ¡mira! (*Abre el libro.*) Es roja por la mañana, a la tarde se pone blanca y se deshoja por la noche.

Cuando se abre en la mañana,
roja como sangre está.
El rocío no la toca
porque se teme quemar.
Abierta en el mediodía
es dura como el coral.
El sol se asoma a los vidrios

HOUSEKEEPER. No mother and father, not even a puppy of her own. But an aunt and uncle made in heaven! (*She embraces the* AUNT.)

UNCLE (*off*). This is too much!

AUNT. Mother of God!

UNCLE. They can trample on my seeds if they wish! But to pull the leaves from the rosebush I love! It's intolerable! It means more to me than the musk rose, hispid, pompon, damask or the Queen Elizabeth eglantine put together. (*To the* AUNT.) Come, come! Look at the damage!

AUNT. Is it ruined?

UNCLE. Fortunately not. But it could have been.

HOUSEKEEPER. We'll never hear the end of it!

UNCLE. I wonder who knocked it over?

HOUSEKEEPER. Don't look at me!

UNCLE. Well it certainly wasn't me.

HOUSEKEEPER. Then it might have been a cat, or a dog, or even a gust of wind.

AUNT. Come along, just clear up the mess!

HOUSEKEEPER. You see how I'm never allowed to give an opinion!

She leaves.

UNCLE (*entering*). It's a rose you've not yet seen. I've grown it as a surprise for you. To tell the truth, the *rosa declinata* is itself an amazing flower with its drooping buds. And the *inermis*, you know, doesn't have a single thorn – quite astonishing! Then there's the Belgian *myrtifolia*, and the *sulfurata* that glows in the dark. But this one is truly unique. Botanists call it the *rosa mutabilis*, which means that it changes. Look! There's a description of it here, together with a picture. (*He opens a book.*) Red in the morning, by evening white, and after dark its petals begin to fall. (*Reading:*)

She opens in the morning,
Her colour the deepest red.
Afraid of being burnt by her,
The dew has quickly fled.
By noon her petals, open wide,
Have all the firmness of coral.
The jealous sun looks down upon

para verla relumbrar.
Cuando en las ramas empiezan
los pájaros a cantar
y se desmaya la tarde
en las violetas del mar,
se pone blanca, con blanco
de una mejilla de sal.
Y cuando toca la noche
blando cuerno de metal
y las estrellas avanzan
mientras los aires se van,
en la raya de lo oscuro,
se comienza a deshojar.

TÍA. ¿Y tiene ya flor?

TÍO. Una que se está abriendo.

TÍA. ¿Dura un día tan sólo?

TÍO. Uno. Pero yo ese día lo pienso pasar al lado para ver cómo se pone blanca.

ROSITA (*entrando*). Mi sombrilla.

TÍO. Su sombrilla.

TÍA (*a voces*). ¡La sombrilla!

AMA (*apareciendo*). ¡Aquí está la sombrilla!

ROSITA *coge la sombrilla y besa a sus tíos.*

ROSITA. ¿Qué tal?

TÍO. Un primor.

TÍA. No hay otra.

ROSITA (*abriendo la sombrilla*). ¿Y ahora?

AMA. ¡Por Dios, cierra la sombrilla, no se puede abrir bajo techado! ¡Llega la mala suerte!

Por la rueda de San Bartolomé
y la varita de San José
y la santa rama de laurel,
enemigo, retírate
por las cuatro esquinas de Jerusalén.

Ríen todos. El TÍO *sale.*

ROSITA (*cerrando*). ¡Ya está!

AMA. No lo hagas más . . . ¡ca . . . ramba!

The splendour of its rival.
When birds take to the branches
To announce the approach of sleep,
And evening descends upon
The ocean's azure deep,
Then her red grows deadly pale,
Like a cheek by sorrow torn,
And night, approaching softly,
Blows on its metal horn.
The stars advance across the sky,
The wind no longer calls,
And on the edge of darkness
Her petals start to fall.

AUNT. Is it flowering yet?

UNCLE. One is beginning to open.

AUNT. And it lasts for just one day?

UNCLE. One day. I intend to sit next to it to observe it turning white.

ROSITA (*entering*). My parasol!

UNCLE. Her parasol!

AUNT (*calling out*). The parasol!

HOUSEKEEPER (*entering*). Her parasol!

ROSITA *takes the parasol and kisses her* AUNT *and* UNCLE.

ROSITA. What do you think?

UNCLE. Exquisite!

AUNT. No one prettier!

ROSITA (*opening the parasol*). And now?

HOUSEKEEPER. For heaven's sake shut it! It will bring bad luck!

By Saint Bartholomew's wheel
And Saint Joseph's holy staff!
By the holy laurel bough,
Evil spirits shall be banned
From Jerusalem's holy land!

They all laugh. The UNCLE *goes out.*

ROSITA (*closing the parasol*). There!

HOUSEKEEPER. Shi . . . Shame on you! Don't ever do that!

ROSITA. ¡Huy!

TÍA. ¿Qué ibas a decir?

AMA. ¡Pero no lo he dicho!

ROSITA (*saliendo con risas*). ¡Hasta luego!

TÍA. ¿Quién te acompaña?

ROSITA (*asomando la cabeza*). Voy con las Manolas.

AMA. Y con el novio.

TÍA. El novio creo que tenía que hacer.

AMA. No sé quién me gusta más, si el novio o ella. (*La* TÍA *se sienta a hacer encaje de bolillos.*) Un par de primos para ponerlos en un vasar de azúcar, y si se murieran, ¡Dios los libre!, embalsamarlos y meterlos en un nicho de cristales y de nieve. ¿A cuál quiere usted más? (*Se pone a limpiar.*)

TÍA. A los dos los quiero como sobrinos.

AMA. Uno por la manta de arriba y otro por la manta de abajo, pero . . .

TÍA. Rosita se crió conmigo . . .

AMA. Claro. Como que yo no creo en la sangre. Para mí esto es ley. La sangre corre por debajo de las venas, pero no se ve. Más se quiere a un primo segundo que se ve todos los días, que a un hermano que está lejos. Por qué, vamos a ver.

TÍA. Mujer, sigue limpiando.

AMA. Ya voy. Aquí no la dejan a una ni abrir los labios. Críe usted una niña hermosa para esto. Déjese usted a sus propios hijos en una chocita temblando de hambre.

TÍA. Será de frío.

AMA. Temblando de todo, para que la digan a una: «¡Cállate!»; y como soy criada no puedo hacer más que callarme, que es lo que hago, y no puedo replicar y decir . . .

TÍA. Y decir ¿qué . . .?

AMA. Que deje usted esos bolillos con ese tiquití, que me va a estallar la cabeza de tiquitís.

TÍA (*riendo*). Mira a ver quién entra.

Hay un silencio en la escena, donde se oye el golpear de los bolillos.

VOZ. ¡¡Manzanillaaaaa finaaa de la sierraa!!

TÍA (*hablando sola*). Es preciso comprar otra vez manzanilla. En algunas ocasiones hace falta . . . Otro día que pase . . ., treinta y siete, treinta y ocho.

ROSITA. Eh?

AUNT. You were going to say?

HOUSEKEEPER. But I didn't say it.

ROSITA (*goes out laughing*). See you later.

AUNT. Who's going with you?

ROSITA (*poking her head around the door*). The Manolas.

HOUSEKEEPER. So where's her young man?

AUNT. I think he's busy.

HOUSEKEEPER. I don't know who I like best – her young man or her. (*The* AUNT *sits to make lace with bobbins.*) A pair of cousins to put on the shelf with the sugar. And if – God forbid – they died, we'd have to embalm them and keep them in a niche in the wall. Which one do you prefer?

AUNT. I love them both, my niece and my nephew.

HOUSEKEEPER. One for the top sheet, one for the bottom. But even so . . .

AUNT. Rosita's grown up with me.

HOUSEKEEPER. Of course she has. That's why I don't believe in blood ties. Blood runs through our veins but we can't see it. But if we see a second cousin all the time, we come to love him more than a brother we hardly ever see. The reason for that . . .

AUNT. Oh, do get on with the cleaning, woman!

HOUSEKEEPER. All right, I shall. I'm not allowed to say a word! I've devoted my life to her for this! And my own children, shivering with hunger in a wretched hovel!

AUNT. I think you mean 'with cold'.

HOUSEKEEPER. Shivering with everything. And then I'm told to shut up and because I'm a servant I have to obey and I can't speak my mind and say . . .

AUNT. What?

HOUSEKEEPER. Stop those bobbins clickety-clacking! My head's going to burst with that clickety-clacking!

AUNT (*laughing*). Go and see who's just arrived.

The stage is in silence except for the sound of the bobbins.

VOICE (*off*). Caaa-mo-mile! Best mountain caaa-mo-mile!

AUNT (*talking to herself*). We need some camomile. It's very useful sometimes. When he comes next . . . thirty-seven, thirty-eight.

VOZ DEL PREGONERO (*muy lejos*). ¡Manzanillaa finaa de la sierraa!

TÍA (*poniendo un alfiler*). Y cuarenta.

SOBRINO (*entrando*). Tía.

TÍA (*sin mirarlo*). Hola, siéntate si quieres. Rosita ya se ha marchado.

SOBRINO. ¿Con quién salió?

TÍA. Con las Manolas. (*Pausa. Mirando al* SOBRINO.) Algo te pasa.

SOBRINO. Sí.

TÍA (*inquieta*). Casi me lo figuro. Ojalá me equivoque.

SOBRINO. No. Lea usted.

TÍA (*lee*). Claro, si es lo natural. Por eso me opuse a tus relaciones con Rosita. Yo sabía que más tarde o más temprano te tendrías que marchar con tus padres. ¡Y que es ahí al lado! Cuarenta días de viaje hacen falta para llegar a Tucumán. Si fuera hombre y joven, te cruzaría la cara.

SOBRINO. Yo no tengo culpa de querer a mi prima. ¿Se imagina usted que me voy con gusto? Precisamente quiero quedarme aquí, y a eso vengo.

TÍA. ¡Quedarte! ¡Quedarte! Tu deber es irte. Son muchas leguas de hacienda y tu padre está viejo. Soy yo la que te tiene que obligar a que tomes el vapor. Pero a mí me dejas la vida amargada. De tu prima no quiero acordarme. Vas a clavar una flecha con cintas moradas sobre su corazón. Ahora se enterará de que las telas no sólo sirven para hacer flores, sino para empapar lágrimas.

SOBRINO. ¿Qué me aconseja usted?

TÍA. Que te vayas. Piensa que tu padre es hermano mío. Aquí no eres más que un paseante de los jardinillos, y allí serás un labrador.

SOBRINO. Pero es que yo quisiera . . .

TÍA. ¿Casarte? ¿Estás loco? Cuando tengas tu porvenir hecho. Y llevarte a Rosita, ¿no? Tendrías que saltar por encima de mí y de tu tío.

SOBRINO. Todo es hablar. Demasiado sé que no puedo. Pero yo quiero que Rosita me espere. Porque volveré pronto.

TÍA. Si antes no pegas la hebra con una tucumana. La lengua se me debió pegar en el cielo de la boca antes de consentir tu noviazgo; porque mi niña se queda sola en estas cuatro paredes, y tú te vas libre por el mar, por aquellos ríos,

VOICE (*off, far away*). Caaa-mo-miiile! Best mountain caaa-mo-miiile!

AUNT (*placing a pin*). Forty!

NEPHEW (*entering*). Aunt . . .

AUNT (*without looking at him*). Come and sit down. Rosita's gone out.

NEPHEW. Who with?

AUNT. Oh, just some friends. (*Pause. Looking at the* NEPHEW.) Something's happened.

NEPHEW. Yes.

AUNT (*uneasily*). I think I can guess. I hope I'm wrong.

NEPHEW. You aren't. Read it.

AUNT (*reads*). It's as I expected. That's why I didn't want you involved with Rosita. I knew that sooner or later you'd have to join your parents. And it's not exactly as if it's next door. Forty days to get to Tucumán! If I were a man and younger than this, I'd smack your face so hard!

NEPHEW. But I'm not to blame for loving Rosita. Do you think I want to leave? I want to stay, which is why I've come to see you.

AUNT. What do you mean 'stay'? It's your duty to go. It's a big estate and your father's getting on. I have to make sure you get on the ship. But you leave me to a life of bitterness. As for Rosita, it doesn't bear thinking about. A poisoned arrow straight through her heart. She'll soon discover that linen may well be for embroidery, but also serves to dry one's tears.

NEPHEW. So what should I do?

AUNT. You have to go. Your father is my brother, after all. Here you simply spend your time admiring the flowers. There you will be a farmer.

NEPHEW. The thing is, I'd really like to . . .

AUNT. Get married? Have you gone mad? When you've sorted out your future. As for taking Rosita with you, over my dead body! And your uncle's!

NEPHEW. It was just an idea. I know that I can't. But I want her to wait for me. I'll be back soon.

AUNT. If you don't meet some girl over there! I should have been struck dumb before agreeing to the engagement. Now my child will be left alone between these walls, while you are free to sail the seas and rivers, to ride through grapefruit

por aquellos bosques de toronjas, y mi niña aquí, un día
igual a otro, y tú allí: el caballo y la escopeta para tirar al
faisán.

SOBRINO. No hay motivo para que me hable usted de esa
manera. Yo di mi palabra y la cumpliré. Por cumplir su
palabra está mi padre en América y usted sabe . . .

TÍA (*suave*). Calla.

SOBRINO. Callo. Pero no confunda usted el respeto con la falta
de vergüenza.

TÍA (*con ironía andaluza*). ¡Perdona, perdona! Se me había
olvidado que ya eras un hombre.

AMA (*entra llorando*). Si fuera un hombre, no se iría.

TÍA (*enérgica*). ¡Silencio!

El AMA *llora con grandes sollozos.*

SOBRINO. Volveré dentro de unos instantes. Dígaselo usted.

TÍA. Descuida. Los viejos son los que tienen que llevar los
malos ratos.

Sale el SOBRINO.

AMA. ¡Ay, qué lástima de mi niña! ¡Ay, qué lastima! ¡Ay, qué
lástima! ¡Éstos son los hombres de ahora! Pidiendo ochavitos
por las calles me quedo yo al lado de esta prenda. Otra vez
vienen los llantos a esta casa. ¡Ay, señora! (*Reaccionando.*)
¡Ojalá se lo coma la serpiente del mar!

TÍA. ¡Dios dirá!

AMA.
Por el ajonjolí,
por las tres santas preguntas
y la flor de la canela,
tenga malas noches
y malas sementeras.
Por el pozo de San Nicolás
se le vuelva veneno la sal.

Coge un jarro de agua y hace una cruz en el suelo.

TÍA. No maldigas. Vete a tu hacienda.

Sale el AMA. *Se oyen risas. La* TÍA *se va.*

MANOLA 1a (*entrando y cerrando la sombrilla*). ¡Ay!

groves. My child here, each day the same, and you there, riding out to shoot pheasants!

NEPHEW. You've no reason to talk to me like this. I gave her my word. I shall honour it. That's why my father went to South America . . . to honour his word, and . . .

AUNT (*gently*). Lower your voice!

NEPHEW. All right. But don't confuse respect with shamelessness.

AUNT (*with irony*). Oh, I do apologise! I'd quite forgotten you're a man now.

HOUSEKEEPER (*enters weeping*). If he were a man, he wouldn't be leaving!

AUNT (*sternly*). Be quiet!

The HOUSEKEEPER *weeps loudly.*

NEPHEW. I'll be back in a minute. Perhaps you'll tell her.

AUNT. Oh, don't you worry. Old people are always the ones to cope with life's worst moments.

The NEPHEW *goes out.*

HOUSEKEEPER. Oh, what a sorry state of affairs! My poor child! This is what men are like today. I'll look after my precious girl even if I have to beg in the streets. Tears have come to this house again. Oh, señora! (*Strongly.*) Let a sea-serpent swallow him alive!

AUNT. God will decide.

HOUSEKEEPER.
By the sesame seed,
By the three holy questions,
By the cinnamon flower,
Let him have sleepless nights!
Rot the seed that he sows,
And by St Nicholas' well
Let his salt turn to poison.

She takes a jar of water and makes a cross on the ground.

AUNT. Oh, stop all this nonsense. Get on with your work.

The HOUSEKEEPER *leaves. Sound of laughter. The* AUNT *leaves.*

FIRST MANOLA (*entering and closing her parasol*). Ah!

MANOLA 2a (*igual*). ¡Ay, qué fresquito!

MANOLA 3a (*igual*). ¡Ay!

ROSITA (*igual*).
> ¿Para quién son los suspiros
> de mis tres lindas Manolas?

MANOLA 1a.
> Para nadie.

MANOLA 2a.
> Para el viento.

MANOLA 3a.
> Para un galán que me ronda.

ROSITA.
> ¿Qué manos recogerán
> los ayes de vuestra boca?

MANOLA 1a.
> La pared.

MANOLA 2a.
> Cierto retrato.

MANOLA 3a.
> Los encajes de mi colcha.

ROSITA.
> También quiero suspirar.
> ¡Ay, amigas! ¡Ay, Manolas!

MANOLA 1a.
> ¿Quién los recoge?

ROSITA.
> Dos ojos
> que ponen blanca la sombra,
> cuyas pestañas son parras,
> donde se duerme la aurora.
> Y, a pesar de negros, son
> dos tardes con amapolas.

MANOLA 1a.
> ¡Ponle una cinta al suspiro!

MANOLA 2a.
> ¡Ay!

MANOLA 3a.
> Dichosa tú.

MANOLA 1a.
> ¡Dichosa!

SECOND MANOLA (*as above*). Ah! How cool!
THIRD MANOLA (*as above*). Ah!
ROSITA (*as above*).
  So for whom are the sighs
  Of my three pretty friends?
FIRST MANOLA.
  Not for anyone
SECOND MANOLA.
             For the wind, perhaps.
THIRD MANOLA.
  Or a handsome boy who courts me.
ROSITA.
  Whose fingers will pluck
  The sighs from your lips?
FIRST MANOLA.
  Perhaps a wall.
SECOND MANOLA.
             Or a picture.
THIRD MANOLA.
  Or the lace of my bedspread.
ROSITA.
  Oh, my dear friends!
  I want to sigh too.
FIRST MANOLA.
  So who gathers your sighs?
ROSITA.
               Two eyes
  That make the darkness bright,
  Whose lashes are vines
  Where daylight sleeps.
  Two eyes that, though as black as jet,
  Like poppies light the deepest night.
FIRST MANOLA.
  You should tie each sigh with a ribbon.
SECOND MANOLA.
  Oh, yes!
THIRD MANOLA.
           You are so lucky!
FIRST MANOLA.
              So happy!

ROSITA.
No me engañéis, que yo sé
cierto rumor de vosotras.
MANOLA 1a.
Rumores son jaramagos.
MANOLA 2a.
Y estribillos de las olas.
ROSITA.
Lo voy a decir ...
MANOLA 1a.
                    Empieza.
MANOLA 3a.
Los rumores son coronas.
ROSITA.
Granada, calle de Elvira,
donde viven las Manolas,
las que se van a la Alhambra,
las tres y las cuatro solas.
Una vestida de verde,
otra de malva, y la otra,
un corselete escocés
con cintas hasta la cola.
Las que van delante, garzas,
la que va detrás, paloma,
abren por las alamedas
muselinas misteriosas.
¡Ay, qué oscura está la Alhambra!
¿Adonde irán las Manolas
mientras sufren en la umbría
el surtidor y la rosa?
¿Qué galanes las esperan?
¿Bajo qué mirto reposan?
¿Qué manos roban perfumes
a sus dos flores redondas?
Nadie va con ellas, nadie;
dos garzas y una paloma.
Pero en el mundo hay galanes
que se tapan con las hojas.
La catedral ha dejado
bronces que la brisa toma.

ROSITA.
  Don't try to deceive me! I've heard things
  About you too.
FIRST MANOLA.
  Nothing but seeds on the wind.
SECOND MANOLA.
  Or the sound of the waves.
ROSITA.
  Then I'll tell you . . .
FIRST MANOLA.
                Go ahead.
THIRD MANOLA.
  Such stories adorn us like crowns.
ROSITA.
  Granada, Elvira Street,
  There live the girls who tease;
  They visit the Alhambra,
  Alone, in twos or threes.
  The first of them is dressed in green,
  The second in deepest purple;
  The third has a bodice which hugs her tight,
  With ribbons that trail below.
  The two in front are herons,
  The one behind a dove.
  Along the darkened poplar groves
  Mysterious muslins move.
  Oh, how dark the Alhambra is!
  Where do the three girls go,
  While the rose and the leaping fountain
  Suffer in deepest shadow?
  What handsome men await them?
  Beneath which myrtle do they rest?
  Whose hands will steal the perfume
  From the flowers of their breasts?
  No one goes with them, no one;
  Two herons and a dove.
  Amongst the trees are hidden
  Men who could give them love.
  The cathedral lies in darkness
  And the breeze softly sings;

El Genil duerme a sus bueyes
y el Dauro a sus mariposas.
La noche viene cargada
con sus colinas de sombra.
Una enseña los zapatos
entre volantes de blonda;
la mayor abre sus ojos
y la menor los entorna.
¿Quién serán aquellas tres
de alto pecho y larga cola?
¿Por qué agitan los pañuelos?
¿Adónde irán a estas horas?
Granada, calle de Elvira,
donde viven las Manolas,
las que se van a la Alhambra
las tres y las cuatro solas.

MANOLA 1a.
Deja que el rumor extienda
sobre Granada sus olas.

MANOLA 2a.
¿Tenemos novio?

ROSITA.
                         Ninguna.

MANOLA 2a.
¿Digo la verdad?

ROSITA.
                         Sí, toda.

MANOLA 3a.
Encajes de escarcha tienen
nuestras camisas de novia.

ROSITA.
Pero . . .

MANOLA 1a.
                La noche nos gusta.

ROSITA.
Pero . . .

MANOLA 2a.
                Por calles en sombra.

MANOLA 1a.
Nos subimos a la Alhambra

The Genil lulls the oxen,
The Dauro butterflies' wings.
Night approaches slowly,
Shadows upon its face;
A girl displays a pretty shoe
Through petticoats of lace.
The eyes of the eldest open wide,
The youngest half-closed in dream;
High-breasted girls, their dresses long,
Who are they, what does it mean?
Handkerchiefs flutter in the wind;
Where, so late, have they been?
Granada, Elvira Street,
There live the girls who tease;
Who visit the Alhambra,
Alone, in twos or threes.

FIRST MANOLA.
  Let the gossip send out
  Its ripples across Granada.

SECOND MANOLA.
  So, do we have a lover?

ROSITA.
                    No, none of you.

SECOND MANOLA.
  Do you want the truth?

ROSITA.
                    Yes.

THIRD MANOLA.
  Our bridal petticoats
  Are edged with frost.

ROSITA.
  But . . .

FIRST MANOLA.
        We welcome the darkness.

ROSITA.
  But . . .

SECOND MANOLA.
        The streets lost in shadow.

FIRST MANOLA.
  We go up to the Alhambra,

las tres y las cuatro solas.

MANOLA 3a.

¡Ay!

MANOLA 2a.

Calla.

MANOLA 3a.

¿Por qué?

MANOLA 2a.

¡Ay!

MANOLA 1a.

¡Ay, sin que nadie lo oiga!

ROSITA.

Alhambra, jazmín de pena
donde la luna reposa.

AMA. Niña, tu tía te llama. (*Muy triste.*)

ROSITA. ¿Has llorado?

AMA (*conteniéndose*). No . . ., es que tengo así, una cosa que . . .

ROSITA. No me asustes. ¿Qué pasa? (*Entra rápida, mirando hacia el* AMA. *Cuando entra* ROSITA, *el* AMA *rompe a llorar en silencio.*)

MANOLA 1a (*en voz alta*). ¿Qué ocurre?

MANOLA 2a. Dinos.

AMA. Callad.

MANOLA 3a (*en voz baja*). ¿Malas noticias?

El AMA *las lleva a la puerta y mira por donde salió* ROSITA.

AMA. ¡Ahora se lo está diciendo!

Pausa, en que todas oyen.

MANOLA 1a. Rosita está llorando, vamos a entrar.

AMA. Venid y os contaré. ¡Dejadla ahora! Podéis salir por el postigo. (*Salen.*)

Queda la escena sola. Un piano lejísimo toca un estudio de Czerny. Pausa. Entra el PRIMO *y al llegar al centro de la habitación, se detiene porque entra* ROSITA. *Quedan los dos mirándose frente a frente. El* PRIMO *avanza. La enlaza por el talle. Ella inclina la cabeza sobre su hombro.*

Alone, in twos or threes.

THIRD MANOLA.
So sad!

SECOND MANOLA.
Hush!

THIRD MANOLA.
But why?

SECOND MANOLA.
So sad!

FIRST MANOLA.
Let no one know our troubles!

ROSITA.
Alhambra of jasmine and anguish,
Where the moon sleeps.

HOUSEKEEPER (*entering sadly*). Child, your aunt wants to speak to you.

ROSITA. Have you been crying?

HOUSEKEEPER (*controlling herself*). No . . . it's just that . . . something . . .

ROSITA. I'm frightened. What's wrong?

> ROSITA *leaves quickly, looking at the* HOUSEKEEPER. *When she has gone, the* HOUSEKEEPER *begins to weep silently.*

FIRST MANOLA (*loudly*). What is it?

SECOND MANOLA. Tell us!

HOUSEKEEPER. Be quiet!

THIRD MANOLA (*quietly*). Bad news?

> *The* HOUSEKEEPER *takes them to the door through which* ROSITA *went out.*

HOUSEKEEPER. She's telling her now.

> *Pause. They all listen.*

FIRST MANOLA. Rosita's crying. Let's go to her.

HOUSEKEEPER. Come with me. I'll tell you what's happened. Leave her for now. You can go out by the side gate.

> *They all exit. The stage is empty. A very distant piano plays a Czerny étude. Pause. The* NEPHEW *enters and stops*

ROSITA.
   ¿Por qué tus ojos traidores
   con los míos se fundieron?
   ¿Por qué tus manos tejieron,
   sobre mi cabeza, flores?
   ¡Qué luto de ruiseñores
   dejas a mi juventud,
   pues siendo norte y salud
   tu figura y tu presencia,
   rompes con tu cruel ausencia
   las cuerdas de mi laúd!

PRIMO (*la lleva a un «vis-á-vis» y se sientan*).
   ¡Ay, prima, tesoro mío,
   ruiseñor en la nevada,
   deja tu boca cerrada
   al imaginario frío!;
   no es de hielo mi desvío,
   que, aunque atraviese la mar,
   el agua me ha de prestar
   nardos de espuma y sosiego
   para contener mi fuego
   cuando me vaya a quemar.

ROSITA.
   Una noche, adormilada
   en mi balcón de jazmines,
   vi bajar dos querubines
   a una rosa enamorada;
   ella se puso encarnada
   siendo blanco su color;
   pero, como tierna flor,
   sus pétalos encendidos
   se fueron cayendo heridos
   por el beso del amor.
   Así yo, primo, inocente,
   en mi jardín de arrayanes,
   daba al aire mis afanes
   y mi blancura a la fuente.
   Tierna gacela imprudente,
   alcé los ojos, te vi
   y en mi corazón sentí
   agujas estremecidas

in the centre of the room when ROSITA *also enters. The two stand face to face. The* NEPHEW *moves towards her. He puts his arm around her waist. She leans her head on his shoulder.*

ROSITA.

Oh, why did our eyes ever meet
If you meant to deceive me?
Why put flowers in my hair?
All I shall hear now is the nightingale's
Sad song, while you, my guiding-star,
The one who gave my life
Its meaning, are leaving me,
Like the strings of a lute struck dumb.

The NEPHEW *takes her over to the 'vis-à-vis'. They sit.*

NEPHEW.

Cousin, you know how much
You mean to me. This isn't coldness.
You have to resist such thoughts.
And at least I know that, when I sail
And my feelings prove too strong,
The calm and beauty of the sea
Will help to give me peace of mind.

ROSITA.

I was half-asleep on my balcony,
And I had a dream in which
Two angels attended a rose that was sick
With love. It was purest white at first,
And then, because of love, bright red.
But finally its petals began to fall.
In the same way I was in
My garden, sharing my longings with
The air, my whiteness reflected in
The water, when suddenly,
Like some timid and innocent doe,
I saw you, and felt at once the pain
Of love opening the wound, red as wallflower.

que me están abriendo heridas
rojas como el alhelí.

PRIMO.

He de volver, prima mía,
para llevarte a mi lado
en barco de oro cuajado,
con las velas de alegría;
luz y sombra, noche y día,
solo pensaré en quererte.

ROSITA.

Pero el veneno que vierte
amor, sobre el alma sola,
tejerá con tierra y ola
el vestido de mi muerte.

PRIMO.

Cuando mi caballo lento
coma tallos con rocío,
cuando la niebla del río
empañe el muro del viento,
cuando el verano violento
ponga el llano carmesí
y la escarcha deje en mí
alfileres de lucero,
te digo, porque te quiero,
que me moriré por ti.

ROSITA.

Yo ansío verte llegar
una tarde por Granada
con toda la luz salada
por la nostalgia del mar;
amarillo limonar,
jazminero desangrado,
por las piedras enredado,
impedirán tu camino,
y nardos en remolino
pondrán loco mi tejado.
¿Volverás?

PRIMO.

Sí. ¡Volveré!

NEPHEW.

   I promise I shall come back,
   And I'll take you with me.
   Imagine a ship of bright gold,
   Its sails of pure joy.
   And before I do,
   I'll think of you day and night.

ROSITA.

   When someone is left
   Behind, love drips
   Its poison slowly.
   My shroud shall be made
   From earth and water.

NEPHEW.

   Whenever my horse grazes
   On grass wet with dew,
   Or the mist from the river
   Forms a wall against
   The wind, or the heat of
   Of summer turns the plain
   Crimson, or I feel
   The sting of the frost's
   Sharp needles, I shall
   Be thinking of you.

ROSITA.

   I long to see you
   Return to Granada
   As evening falls,
   When the light is full of salt
   From longing for
   The sea. But lemon groves
   And bloodless jasmine,
   Entangled with stones,
   Will block the way.
   I doubt you will ever
   Come back.

NEPHEW.

   You have my word.

ROSITA.

¿Qué paloma iluminada me anunciará tu llegada?

PRIMO.

El palomo de mi fe.

ROSITA.

Mira que yo bordaré
sábanas para los dos.

PRIMO.

Por los diamantes de Dios y el clavel de su costado,
juro que vendré a tu lado.

ROSITA.

¡Adiós, primo!

PRIMO.

¡Prima, adiós!

Se abrazan en el «vis-à-vis». Lejos se oye el piano. El
PRIMO *sale.* ROSITA *queda llorando. Aparece el* TÍO, *que*
cruza la escena hacia el invernadero. Al ver a su TÍO,
ROSITA *coge el libro de las rosas que está al alcance de su*
mano.

TÍO.

¿Qué hacías?

ROSITA.

Nada.

TÍO. ¿Estabas leyendo?

ROSITA. Sí.

Sale el TÍO. *Leyendo.*

Cuando se abre en la mañana
roja como sangre está;
el rocío no la toca
porque se teme quemar.
Abierta en el mediodía
es dura como el coral.
El sol se asoma a los vidrios
para verla relumbrar.
Cuando en las ramas empiezan
los pájaros a cantar
y se desmaya la tarde

ROSITA.
Perhaps a white dove will bring me news.
NEPHEW.
The proof of my love.
ROSITA.
Then I'll embroider sheets for us.
NEPHEW.
I swear in God's name.
By the wounds of our Lord.
ROSITA.
Then God go with you.
NEPHEW.
                    And God be with you.

They embrace on the 'vis-à-vis'. The piano is heard in the distance. The NEPHEW *leaves.* ROSITA *is left weeping. The* UNCLE *enters and crosses the stage towards the greenhouse. When she sees him,* ROSITA *picks up the rose book, which is nearby.*

UNCLE. What were you doing?
ROSITA. Nothing.
UNCLE. Reading?

The UNCLE *leaves.* ROSITA *reads aloud from the book.*

ROSITA.
She opens in the morning,
Her colour the deepest red.
Afraid of being burnt by her,
The dew has quickly fled.
By noon her petals, open wide,
Have all the firmness of coral.
The jealous sun looks down upon
The splendour of its rival.
When birds take to the branches
To announce the approach of sleep,
And evening descends upon
The ocean's azure deep,

en las violetas del mar,
se pone blanca, con blanco
de una mejilla de sal;
y cuando toca la noche
blando cuerno de metal
y las estrellas avanzan
mientras los aires se van,
en la raya de lo oscuro
se comienza a deshojar.

Telón.

Then her red grows deadly pale,
Like a cheek by sorrow torn,
And night, approaching softly,
Blows on its metal horn.
The stars advance across the sky,
The wind no longer calls,
And on the edge of darkness
Her petals start to fall.

Curtain.

Acto segundo

Salón de la casa de DOÑA ROSITA. *Al fondo, el jardín.*

EL SEÑOR X. Pues yo siempre seré de este siglo.

TÍO. El siglo que acabamos de empezar será un siglo materialista.

EL SEÑOR X. Pero de mucho más adelanto que el que se fue. Mi amigo, el señor Longoria, de Madrid, acaba de comprar un automóvil con el que se lanza a la fantástica velocidad de treinta kilómetros por hora; y el Sha de Persia, que por cierto es un hombre muy agradable, ha comprado también un Panhard Levassor de veinti-cuatro caballos.

TÍO. Y digo yo: ¿adónde van con tanta prisa? Ya ve usted lo que ha pasado en la carrera París–Madrid, que ha habido que suspenderla, porque antes de llegar a Burdeos se mataron todos los corredores.

EL SEÑOR X. El conde Zboronsky, muerto en el accidente, y Marcel Renault, o Renol, que de ambas maneras suele y puede decirse, muerto también en el accidente, son mártires de la ciencia que serán puestos en los altares el día en que venga la religión de lo positivo. A Renol le conocí bastante. ¡Pobre Marcelo!

TÍO. No me convencerá usted. (*Se sienta.*)

EL SEÑOR X (*con el pie puesto en la silla y jugando con el bastón*). Superlativamente; aunque un catedrático de Economía Política no puede discutir con un cultivador de rosas. Pero hoy día, créame usted, no privan los quietismos ni las ideas *oscurantistas.* Hoy día se abren camino un Juan Bautista Say o Se, que de ambas maneras suele y puede decirse, o un conde León Tolstuá, vulgo Tolstoi, tan galán en la forma como profundo en el concepto. Yo me siento en la Polis viviente; no soy partidario de la Natura Naturata.

TÍO. Cada uno vive como puede o como sabe en esta vida diaria.

EL SEÑOR X. Está entendido, la Tierra es un planeta mediocre, pero hay que ayudar a la civilización. Si Santos Dumont, en vez de estudiar Meteorología comparada, se hubiera

Act Two

The drawing room in ROSITA*'s house. The garden in the background.*

MR X. I shall always be a man of this century.

UNCLE. The century we've just begun will be pure materialism.

MR X. But much more progressive than that just ended. My friend, Mr Longoria, from Madrid, has just bought a motor car. It hurtles along at the incredible speed of thirty kilometres an hour. And the Shah of Persia – a quite delightful fellow – has acquired a twenty-four-horsepower Panhard-Levassor.

UNCLE. I'd like to know why everyone's in such a hurry. You saw what happened in the Paris–Madrid rally. They had to abandon it. All the drivers were dead before they reached Bordeaux.

MR X. Count Zboronsky among them, and Marcel Renault too – you can pronounce it as Renol as well, you know. Both martyrs to science. They will both become saints the day that the religion of positivism dawns. I knew Renol well. Poor Marcel!

UNCLE. You will never convince me!

The UNCLE *sits down.*

MR X (*a foot on a chair and playing with his cane*). I shall do so brilliantly, though a professor of Political Economy shouldn't really be talking to a rose-grower. You take my word for it: nowadays there is no place for quietist attitudes or obscurantist ideas. The way ahead lies in the hands of Jean-Baptiste Say, or Se as he is often correctly called, or Count Leo Tolstwa, vulgarly Tolstoy, as elegant in form as profound in concept. I support the current polity. I do not believe in *natura naturata*.

UNCLE. Everyone lives his life as best he can or best knows how.

MR X. It goes without saying, this Earth of ours is decidedly mediocre, but one has to give it a helping hand. Now if Santos Dumont, instead of studying comparative

dedicado a cuidar rosas, el aeróstato dirigible estaría en el seno de Brahma.

TÍO (*disgustado*). La botánica también es una ciencia.

EL SEÑOR X (*despectivo*). Sí, pero aplicada: para estudiar jugos de la *anthemis* olorosa, o el ruibarbo, o la enorme *pulsátila*, o el narcótico de la *datura stramonium*.

TÍO (*ingenuo*). ¿Le interesan a usted esas plantas?

EL SEÑOR X. No tengo el suficiente volumen de experiencia sobre ellas. Me interesa la cultura, que es distinto. *¡Voilà!* (*Pausa.*) ¿Y . . . Rosita?

TÍO. ¿Rosita? (*Pausa. En alta voz.*) ¡Rosita! . . .

VOZ (*dentro*). No está.

TÍO. No está.

EL SEÑOR X. Lo siento.

TÍO. Yo también. Como es su santo, habrá salido a rezar los cuarenta credos.

EL SEÑOR X. Le entrega usted de mi parte este *pendentif*. Es una Torre Eiffel de nácar sobre dos palomas que llevan en sus picos la rueda de la industria.

TÍO. Lo agradecerá mucho.

EL SEÑOR X. Estuve por haberla traído un cañoncito de plata por cuyo agujero se veía la Virgen de Lurdes, o Lourdes, o una hebilla para el cinturón hecha con una serpiente y cuatro libélulas, pero preferí lo primero por ser de más gusto.

TÍO. Gracias.

EL SEÑOR X. Encantado de su favorable acogida.

TÍO. Gracias.

EL SEÑOR X. Póngame a los pies de su señora esposa.

TÍO. Muchas gracias.

EL SEÑOR X. Póngame a los pies de su encantadora sobrinita, a la que deseo venturas en su celebrado onomástico.

TÍO. Mil gracias.

EL SEÑOR X. Considéreme seguro servidor suyo.

TÍO. Un millón de gracias.

EL SEÑOR X. Vuelvo a repetir . . .

TÍO. Gracias, gracias, gracias.

EL SEÑOR X. Hasta siempre. (*Se va.*)

TÍO (*a voces*). Gracias, gracias, gracias.

AMA (*sale riendo*). No sé cómo tiene usted paciencia. Con este señor y con el otro, don Confucio Montes de Oca,

meteorology, had devoted his life to the cultivation of roses, the navigable airship would still be in the bosom of Brahma.

UNCLE (*annoyed*). Botany is a science, you know.

MR X (*disparagingly*). Indeed, but an applied science: for studying the juices of the fragrant *Anthemis*, or rhubarb, or the giant *pulsatilla*, or the narcotic content of the *datura stramonium*.

UNCLE (*innocently*). You take an interest in such plants?

MR X. I lack sufficient volume of experience in the field. What interests me is culture, which is quite a different matter. Voilà! (*Pause.*) . . . Is Rosita at home?

UNCLE. Rosita? (*Pause. Calls out.*) Rosita!

VOICE (*off*). No, she isn't!

UNCLE. No, she isn't.

MR X. A pity.

UNCLE. Yes, indeed. It's her saint's day, you see. She'll have gone to say her forty prayers.

MR X. Would you give her this pendant on my behalf? It's a mother-of-pearl Eiffel Tower over two doves who bear in their beaks the wheel of industry.

UNCLE. She will be grateful.

MR X. I was rather tempted to give her a small silver cannon through whose mouth one could see the Virgin of Lourdes, or Lurdes, or a buckle for a belt composed of a serpent and four dragonflies. But the first seemed to be in better taste.

UNCLE. Many thanks.

MR X. Delighted by your warm welcome.

UNCLE. Thank you so much.

MR X. My humble respects to your dear wife.

UNCLE. Thank you again.

MR X. Sincere regards to your charming niece. I wish her the best of fortune on her saint's day.

UNCLE. A thousand thanks.

MR X. Your obedient servant.

UNCLE. A million thanks.

MR X. Let me say once more . . .

UNCLE. Oh, thank you, thank you, thank you.

MR X. I shall say farewell. (*He goes out.*)

UNCLE (*calling after him*). My everlasting thanks to you!

HOUSEKEEPER (*enters laughing*). I don't know where you find the patience. What with this one and the other gentleman –

bautizado en la logia número cuarenta y tres, va a arder la casa un día.

TÍO. Te he dicho que no me gusta que escuches las conversaciones.

AMA. Eso se llama ser desagradecido. Estaba detrás de la puerta, sí, señor, pero no era para oír, sino para poner una escoba boca arriba y que el señor se fuera.

TÍA. ¿Se fue ya?

TÍO. Ya. (*Entra.*)

AMA. ¿También éste pretende a Rosita?

TÍA. Pero ¿por qué hablas de pretendientes? ¡No conoces a Rosita!

AMA. Pero conozco a los pretendientes.

TÍA. Mi sobrina está comprometida.

AMA. No me haga usted hablar, no me haga usted hablar, no me haga usted hablar, no me haga usted hablar.

TÍA. Pues cállate.

AMA. ¿A usted le parece bien que un hombre se vaya y deje quince años plantada a una mujer que es la flor de la manteca? Ella debe casarse. Ya me duelen las manos de guardar mantelerías de encaje de Marsella y juegos de cama adornados de guipure y caminos de mesa y cubrecamas de gasa con flores de realce. Es que ya debe usarlos y romperlos, pero ella no se da cuenta de cómo pasa el tiempo. Tendrá el pelo de plata y todavía estará cosiendo cintas de raso liberti en los volantes de su camisa de novia.

TÍA. Pero ¿por qué te metes en lo que no te importa?

AMA (*con asombro*). Pero si no me meto, es que estoy metida.

TÍA. Yo estoy segura de que ella es feliz.

AMA. Se lo figura. Ayer me tuvo todo el día acompañándola en la puerta del circo, porque se empeñó en que uno de los titiriteros se parecía a su primo.

TÍA. ¿Y se parecía realmente?

AMA. Era hermoso como un novicio cuando sale a cantar la primera misa, pero ya quisiera su sobrino tener aquel talle, aquel cuello de nácar y aquel bigote. No se parecía nada. En la familia de ustedes no hay hombres guapos.

TÍA. ¡Gracias, mujer!

AMA. Son todos bajos y un poquito caídos de hombros.

that Don Confucius Montes de Oca, confirmed in Lodge number 43 – this house will soon go up in flames!

UNCLE. I've told you before not to eavesdrop!

HOUSEKEEPER. Now there's gratitude for you! I admit I was behind the door, sir, but not to listen – only to put a broom upside down so the gentleman would leave.

AUNT (*entering*). Has he gone?

UNCLE (*leaving*). This very minute.

HOUSEKEEPER. Is *he* courting Rosita too?

AUNT. What do you mean? You obviously don't know Rosita.

HOUSEKEEPER. But I *do* know her suitors.

AUNT. My niece is engaged.

HOUSEKEEPER. Don't make me say it! Don't make me say it! Don't make me say it!

AUNT. Then don't say it!

HOUSEKEEPER. But is it right for a man to go off for fifteen years and leave behind a girl who's the cream on the butter? She should get married. My hands are aching from putting away so many lace tablecloths, embroidered sheets and pillowcases, table-mats, and lacy bedspreads decorated with flowers. She ought to be using them, wearing them out. She doesn't seem to know that time is passing. She'll have hair like silver and still she'll be sewing satin ribbons on the frills of her honeymoon nightdress.

AUNT. Don't get involved in things that don't concern you.

HOUSEKEEPER (*astonished*). I don't get involved. I *am* involved!

AUNT. I'm sure she's happy.

HOUSEKEEPER. She thinks she is. Yesterday she made me wait all day with her at the entrance to the circus. She insisted that one of the puppeteers looked like her cousin.

AUNT. And did he?

HOUSEKEEPER. He was as handsome as a young priest saying his first mass. But as for your nephew, he'd give anything to have that waist, that lovely throat, that smart moustache. No, he wasn't like him, not one bit. There aren't any handsome men in your family.

AUNT. Oh, it's very nice of you to say so.

HOUSEKEEPER. They're all so short . . . and a bit round-shouldered.

TÍA. ¡Vaya!

AMA. Es la pura verdad, señora. Lo que pasó es que a Rosita le
gustó el saltimbanqui, como me gustó a mí y como le gustaría
a usted. Pero ella lo achaca todo al otro. A veces me gustaría
tirarle un zapato a la cabeza. Porque de tanto mirar al cielo
se le van a poner los ojos de vaca.

TÍA. Bueno; y punto final. Bien está que la zafia hable, pero que
no ladre.

AMA. No me echará usted en cara que no la quiero.

TÍA. A veces me parece que no.

AMA. El pan me quitaría de la boca y la sangre de mis venas, si
ella me los deseara.

TÍA (*fuerte*). ¡Pico de falsa miel! ¡Palabras!

AMA (*fuerte*). ¡Y hechos! Lo tengo demostrado, ¡y hechos! La
quiero más que usted.

TÍA. Eso es mentira.

AMA(*fuerte*). ¡Eso es verdad!

TÍA. ¡No me levantes la voz!

AMA (*alto*). Para eso tengo la campanilla de la lengua.

TÍA. ¡Cállate, mal educada!

AMA. Cuarenta años llevo al lado de usted.

TÍA (*casi llorando*). ¡Queda usted despedida!

AMA (*fortísimo*). ¡Gracias a Dios que la voy a perder de
vista!

TÍA (*llorando*). ¡A la calle inmediatamente!

AMA (*rompiendo a llorar*). ¡A la calle!

> *Se dirige llorando a la puerta y al entrar se le cae un objeto.*
> *Las dos están llorando.*

> *Pausa.*

TÍA (*limpiándose las lágrimas y dulcemente*). ¿Qué se te ha
caído?

AMA (*llorando*). Un portatermómetro, estilo Luis Quince.

TÍA. ¿Sí?

AMA. Sí, señora. (*Lloran.*)

TÍA. ¿A ver?

AMA. Para el santo de Rosita. (*Se acerca.*)

TÍA (*sorbiendo*). Es una preciosidad.

AUNT. Go on with you!

HOUSEKEEPER. It's the honest truth, señora. And then Rosita took a fancy to the acrobat . . . and so did I, and you would have too. But she always thinks her cousin's like them. I'd like to throw a shoe at her head at times. She stares into space so much, she'll soon have eyes like a cow.

AUNT. All right, that's quite enough! Clowns may speak, but they shouldn't bark.

HOUSEKEEPER. You'll be telling me next that I don't love her.

AUNT. I do wonder sometimes.

HOUSEKEEPER. I'd give her the bread from my mouth and the blood from my veins if she needed them.

AUNT (*strongly*). Oh, very fine words! Sweet as sugar!

HOUSEKEEPER (*strongly*). Actions speak louder than words. I've proved it. I love her more than you!

AUNT. That's not true.

HOUSEKEEPER. It *is* true!

AUNT. Don't you dare raise your voice to me!

HOUSEKEEPER (*loudly*). That's what my tongue is for!

AUNT. Be quiet, you ill-mannered woman!

HOUSEKEEPER. Forty years I've worked for you!

AUNT (*almost crying*). You are dismissed!

HOUSEKEEPER (*still louder*). Thank God I'll never see you again!

AUNT (*crying*). Get out! At once!

HOUSEKEEPER (*bursting into tears*). I'm going!

She goes to the door in tears. As she is about to exit, she drops something. Both women are in tears.

Pause.

AUNT (*wiping away her tears, speaking gently*). What's that?

HOUSEKEEPER (*weeping*). A thermometer-case, in the style of Louis the fifteenth.

AUNT. Really?

HOUSEKEEPER. Yes, señora.

Both weeping.

AUNT. Let me see.

HOUSEKEEPER (*approaching*). It's for Rosita's saint's day.

AUNT (*sniffing*). It's really lovely.

AMA (*con voz de llanto*). En medio del terciopelo hay una fuente hecha con caracoles de verdad; sobre la fuente, una glorieta de alambre con rosas verdes; el agua de la taza es un grupo de lentejuelas azules y el surtidor es el propio termómetro. Los charcos que hay alrededor están pintados al aceite y encima de ellos bebe un ruiseñor todo bordado con hilo de oro. Yo quise que tuviera cuerda y cantara, pero no pudo ser.

TÍA. No pudo ser.

AMA. Pero no hace falta que cante. En el jardín los tenemos vivos.

TÍA. Es verdad. (*Pausa.*) ¿Para qué te has metido en esto?

AMA (*llorando*). Yo doy todo lo que tengo por Rosita.

TÍA. ¡Es que tú la quieres como nadie!

AMA. Pero después que usted.

TÍA. No. Tú le has dado tu sangre.

AMA. Usted le ha sacrificado su vida.

TÍA. Pero yo lo he hecho por deber y tú por generosidad.

AMA (*más fuerte*). ¡No diga usted eso!

TÍA. Tú has demostrado quererla más que nadie.

AMA. Yo he hecho lo que haría cualquiera en mi caso. Una criada. Ustedes me pagan y yo sirvo.

TÍA. Siempre te hemos considerado como de la familia.

AMA. Una humilde criada que da lo que tiene y nada más.

TÍA. Pero ¿me vas a decir que nada más?

AMA. ¿Y soy otra cosa?

TÍA (*irritada*). Eso no lo puedes decir aquí. Me voy por no oírte.

AMA (*irritada*). Y yo también. (*Salen rápidas una por cada puerta. Al salir, la* TÍA *se tropieza con el* TÍO.)

TÍO. De tanto vivir juntas, los encajes se os hacen espinas.

TÍA. Es que quiere salirse siempre con la suya.

TÍO. No me expliques, ya me lo sé todo de memoria . . . Y sin embargo no puedes estar sin ella. Ayer oí cómo le explicabas con todo detalle nuestra cuenta corriente en el Banco. No te sabes quedar en tu sitio. No me parece conversación lo más a propósito para una criada.

TÍA. Ella no es una criada.

HOUSEKEEPER (*weepy*). In the middle of the velvet there's a fountain of real shells. Above the fountain there's an arbour made of wire and green roses. The water in the basin is a cluster of blue sequins, and the water-jet is the thermometer itself. The pools are painted in oil and there's a nightingale drinking, embroidered in gold thread. I wanted one you could wind up so it would sing, but I couldn't find one.

AUNT. Oh, dear!

HOUSEKEEPER. Still, it doesn't have to sing. We've got real birds in the garden.

AUNT. Of course we have! (*Pause.*) But why spend so much money?

HOUSEKEEPER (*weeping*). Because what is mine is Rosita's.

AUNT. You really love her more than anyone.

HOUSEKEEPER. Not more than you.

AUNT. Yes you do. You've given her your blood.

HOUSEKEEPER. You've sacrificed your life.

AUNT. Out of duty. But you out of generosity.

HOUSEKEEPER (*strongly*). Don't say that!

AUNT. You've shown you love her more than anyone.

HOUSEKEEPER. I've done what anyone in my place would do. I'm a servant. You pay me and I do what I have to.

AUNT. We've always thought of you as one of the family.

HOUSEKEEPER. I'm only a servant. I do what I can.

AUNT. What do you mean 'only a servant'?

HOUSEKEEPER. What else am I?

AUNT (*annoyed*). How can you say that to me? I shan't listen. I'm going!

HOUSEKEEPER (*annoyed*). I'm going too!

They go out through different doors. As the AUNT *goes out, she bumps into the* UNCLE.

UNCLE. You two have been together for so long, the softest lace becomes a thorn.

AUNT. She always wants the last word.

UNCLE. No need to tell me. I know how it is. But you can't do without her. Why, only yesterday I heard you giving her all the details of our current bank account. You should know better. It's not the kind of thing to be telling a servant.

AUNT. She isn't a servant.

TÍO (*con dulzura*). Basta, basta, no quiero llevarte la contraria.

TÍA. Pero ¿es que conmigo no se puede hablar?

TÍO. Se puede, pero yo prefiero callarme.

TÍA. Aunque te quedes con tus palabras de reproche.

TÍO. ¿Para qué voy a decir nada a estas alturas? Por no discutir soy capaz de hacerme la cama, de limpiar mis trajes con jabón de palo y cambiar las alfombras de mi habitación.

TÍA. No es justo que te des ese aire de hombre superior y mal servido, cuando todo en esta casa está supeditado a tu comodidad y a tus gustos.

TÍO (*dulce*). Al contrario, hija.

TÍA (*seria*). Completamente. En vez de hacer encajes, podo las plantas. ¿Qué haces tú por mí?

TÍO. Perdona. Llega un momento en que las personas que viven juntas muchos años hacen motivo de disgusto y de inquietud las cosas más pequeñas, para poner intensidad y afanes en lo que está definitivamente muerto. Con veinte años no teníamos estas conversaciones.

TÍA. No. Con veinte años se rompían los cristales . . .

TÍO. Y el frío era un juguete en nuestras manos.

> *Aparece* ROSITA. *Viene vestida de rosa. Ya la moda ha cambiado de mangas de jamón a 1900. Falda en forma de campanela. Atraviesa la escena, rápida, con unas tijeras en la mano. En el centro se para.*

ROSITA. ¿Ha llegado el cartero?

TÍO. ¿Ha llegado?

TÍA. No sé. (*A voces.*) ¿Ha llegado el cartero? (*Pausa.*) No, todavía no.

ROSITA. Siempre pasa a estas horas.

TÍO. Hace rato debió llegar.

TÍA. Es que muchas veces se entretiene.

ROSITA. El otro día me lo encontré jugando al uni-uni-doli-doli con tres chicos y todo el montón de cartas en el suelo.

TÍA. Ya vendrá.

ROSITA. Avisadme. (*Sale rápida.*)

TÍO. Pero ¿dónde vas con esas tijeras?

ROSITA. Voy a cortar unas rosas.

TÍO (*asombrado*). ¿Cómo? ¿Y quién te ha dado permiso?

UNCLE (*gently*). All right, all right, I don't want to argue.

AUNT. You can say whatever you like to me!

UNCLE. Of course I can. But I'd rather not.

AUNT. You'd rather bottle it up inside!

UNCLE. What's the point of discussing it? I prefer a bit of peace and quiet – make my bed, wash my suits, rearrange the rugs in my room.

AUNT. You aren't being fair at all, pretending to be someone superior, neglected by the rest of us. Not when everything in the house takes second place to your comfort and convenience.

UNCLE (*gently*). I rather think it's the other way round.

AUNT (*seriously*). I disagree. I ought to be making lace, but what am I doing? Pruning plants! And what do you do for me?

UNCLE. The fact is, my dear, when two people have been together for many years, they get worked up at the least excuse. It's their way of breathing new life into something that is, quite frankly, dead. We never had these arguments when we were twenty.

AUNT. No, then we used to make the windows rattle . . .

UNCLE. And the cold was a toy to amuse us.

> ROSITA *enters. She is dressed in pink. The style has changed from leg-of-mutton sleeves to that of 1900. Her skirt is bell-shaped. She crosses the stage quickly with a pair of scissors and stops centre stage.*

ROSITA. Has the postman been?

UNCLE. Has he been?

AUNT. I don't know. (*Calling out.*) Has the postman been? (*Pause.*) No, not yet.

ROSITA. He always comes around this time.

UNCLE. He should have come by now.

AUNT. He sometimes takes his time.

ROSITA. I saw him the other day playing hopscotch with three children. All the letters were on the floor in a great pile.

AUNT. I expect he'll soon be here.

ROSITA. Let me know when he comes. (*Goes out quickly.*)

UNCLE. What are you doing with those scissors?

ROSITA. I'm going to cut some roses.

UNCLE (*taken aback*). What? Who gave you permission?

TÍA. Yo. Es el día de su santo.

ROSITA. Quiero poner en las jardineras y en el florero de la entrada.

TÍO. Cada vez que cortáis una rosa es como si me cortaseis un dedo. Ya sé que es igual. (*Mirando a su mujer.*) No quiero discutir. Sé que duran poco. (*Entra el* AMA.) Así lo dice el vals de las rosas, que es una de las composiciones más bonitas de estos tiempos, pero no puedo reprimir el disgusto que me produce verlas en los búcaros. (*Sale de escena.*)

ROSITA (*al* AMA). ¿Vino el correo?

AMA. Pues para lo único que sirven las rosas es para adornar las habitaciones.

ROSITA (*irritada*). Te he preguntado si ha venido el correo.

AMA (*irritada*). ¿Es que me guardo yo las cartas cuando vienen?

TÍA. Anda, corta las flores.

ROSITA. Para todo hay en esta casa una gotita de acíbar.

AMA. Nos encontramos el rejalgar por los rincones. (*Sale de escena.*)

TÍA. ¿Estás contenta?

ROSITA. No sé.

TÍA. ¿Y eso?

ROSITA. Cuando no veo a la gente estoy contenta, pero como la tengo que ver . . .

TÍA. ¡Claro! No me gusta la vida que llevas. Tu novio no te exige que seas hurona. Siempre me dice en las cartas que salgas.

ROSITA. Pero es que en la calle noto cómo pasa el tiempo y no quiero perder las ilusiones. Ya han hecho otra casa nueva en la placeta. No quiero enterarme de cómo pasa el tiempo.

TÍA. ¡Claro! Muchas veces te he aconsejado que escribas a tu primo y te cases aquí con otro. Tú eres alegre. Yo sé que hay muchachos y hombres maduros enamorados de ti.

ROSITA. ¡Pero, tía! Tengo las raíces muy hondas, muy bien hincadas en mi sentimiento. Si no viera a la gente, me creería que hace una semana que se marchó. Yo espero como el

AUNT. I did. It's her saint's day.

ROSITA. I want to put some in the vases, and in the hall.

UNCLE. Whenever you cut a rose, I feel as if I've lost a finger! It's exactly the same. (*Looking at his wife.*) But I'm not going to argue. They don't last long anyway. (*The* HOUSEKEEPER *enters.*) As the 'Waltz of the Roses' has it. It's one of the most beautiful modern songs, you know. But the sight of roses in vases really upsets me!

The UNCLE *exits.*

ROSITA (*to the* HOUSEKEEPER). Any sign of the postman?

HOUSEKEEPER. What good are roses except to make rooms look pretty?

ROSITA (*annoyed*). I asked you if there's any sign of the postman?

HOUSEKEEPER (*annoyed*). Do you think I keep the letters when they come?

AUNT. Off you go now. Cut the flowers.

ROSITA. In this house there's always a hint of bitterness.

HOUSEKEEPER. Quite true. A touch of arsenic in every corner.

She leaves.

AUNT. Aren't you happy?

ROSITA. I don't know.

AUNT. What does that mean?

ROSITA. I'm happy enough when I don't see people, but since I can't avoid them . . .

AUNT. Of course you can't. I don't like the kind of life you are leading. Your fiancé doesn't want you to shut yourself away. In his letters to me he says he wants you to go out.

ROSITA. It's just that when I go out I can see how time is passing. And I don't want my hopes dashed. There's a new house been built in the little square. I don't want to know that time is passing me by!

AUNT. I agree with you. I've told you often enough. You should write to him and tell him you want to marry someone here. You are full of life. There are lots of men who fancy you, young and not so young.

ROSITA. But, Aunt, the roots of my love for him have gone so deep. If other people weren't a constant reminder, it would seem no more than a week since he left. I wait for him now

primer día. Además, ¿qué es un año, ni dos, ni cinco? (*Suena una campanilla.*) El correo.

TÍA. ¿Qué te habrá mandado?

AMA (*entrando en escena*). Ahí están las solteronas cursilonas.

TÍA. ¡María Santísima!

ROSITA. Que pasen.

AMA. La madre y las tres niñas. Lujo por fuera y para la boca unas malas migas de maíz. ¡Qué azotazo en el . . . les daba . . .! (*Sale de escena.*)

Entran las tres cursilonas y su mamá. Las tres SOLTERONAS *vienen con inmensos sombreros de plumas malas, trajes exageradísimos, guantes hasta el codo con pulseras encima y abanicos pendientes de largas cadenas. La* MADRE *viste de negro pardo con un sombrero de viejas cintas moradas.*

MADRE. Felicidades. (*Se besan.*)

ROSITA. Gracias. (*Besa a las* SOLTERONAS.) ¡Amor! ¡Caridad! ¡Clemencia!

SOLTERONA 1a. Felicidades.

SOLTERONA 2a. Felicidades.

SOLTERONA 3a. Felicidades.

TÍA (*a la* Madre). ¿Cómo van esos pies?

MADRE. Cada vez peor. Si no fuera por éstas, estaría siempre en casa. (*Se sientan.*)

TÍA. ¿No se da usted las friegas con alhucemas?

SOLTERONA 1a. Todas las noches.

SOLTERONA 2a. Y el cocimiento de malvas.

TÍA. No hay reúma que resista.

Pausa.

MADRE. ¿Y su esposo?

TÍA. Está bien, gracias.

Pausa.

MADRE. Con sus rosas.

TÍA. Con sus rosas.

SOLTERONA 3a. ¡Qué bonitas son las flores!

SOLTERONA 2a. Nosotras tenemos en una maceta un rosal de San Francisco.

ROSITA. Pero las rosas de San Francisco no huelen.

as I did on the very first day. Anyway, what's a year, or two years, or five? (*A bell rings.*) The postman!

AUNT. I wonder what he's sent you this time.

HOUSEKEEPER (*entering*). It's those show-off spinsters!

AUNT. God save us!

ROSITA. Ask them in.

HOUSEKEEPER. The mother and her three girls. All show and just stale crumbs to keep them going. What they need is a good smack across their . . . (*She goes out.*)

The three pretentious girls enter with their mother. The three SPINSTERS wear enormous hats with tasteless feathers, absurd dresses, elbow-length gloves with bracelets over them, and fans dangling from long chains. The MOTHER wears a faded black dress and a hat with old purple ribbons.

MOTHER (*exchanging kisses with ROSITA*). Felicitations!

ROSITA. Thank you. (*She kisses the SPINSTERS in turn.*) Faith! Charity! Mercy!

FIRST SPINSTER. Felicitations!

SECOND SPINSTER. Felicitations!

THIRD SPINSTER. Felicitations!

AUNT (*to the MOTHER*). How are your feet?

MOTHER. Worse by the day, you know. If it weren't for my girls, I'd never go out. (*They sit down.*)

AUNT. Have you tried rubbing them with lavender?

FIRST SPINSTER. Every night.

SECOND SPINSTER. And boiled mallows.

AUNT. They are very good for rheumatism.

Pause.

MOTHER. How is your husband these days?

AUNT. Quite well, thank you.

Pause.

MOTHER. Still with his roses?

AUNT. Still with his roses.

THIRD SPINSTER. Flowers are so beautiful!

SECOND SPINSTER. We have a St Francis rose-bush in a pot.

ROSITA. But the St Francis rose has no smell.

SOLTERONA 1a. Muy poco.

MADRE. A mí lo que más me gustan son las celindas.

SOLTERONA 3a. Las violetas son también preciosas.

Pausa.

MADRE. Niñas, ¿habéis traído la tarjeta?

SOLTERONA 3a. Sí. Es una niña vestida de rosa, que al mismo tiempo es barómetro. El fraile con la capucha está ya muy visto. Según la humedad, las faldas de la niña, que son de papel finísimo, se abren o se cierran.

ROSITA (*leyendo*).
Una mañana en el campo
cantaban los ruiseñores
y en su cántico decían:
«Rosita, de las mejores».

¿Para qué se han molestado ustedes?

TÍA. Es de mucho gusto.

MADRE. ¡Gusto no me falta, lo que me falta es dinero!

SOLTERONA 1a. ¡Mamá . . .!

SOLTERONA 2a. ¡Mamá . . .!

SOLTERONA 3a. ¡Mamá . . .!

MADRE. Hijas, aquí tengo confianza. No nos oye nadie. Pero usted lo sabe muy bien: desde que faltó mi pobre marido hago verdaderos milagros para administrar la pensión que nos queda. Todavía me parece oír al padre de estas hijas cuando, generoso y caballero como era, me decía: «Enriqueta, gasta, gasta, que ya gano setenta duros»; ¡pero aquellos tiempos pasaron! A pesar de todo, nosotras no hemos descendido de clase. ¡Y qué angustias he pasado, señora, para que estas hijas puedan seguir usando sombrero! ¡Cuántas lágrimas, cuántas tristezas por una cinta o un grupo de bucles! Esas plumas y esos alambres me tienen costado muchas noches en vela.

SOLTERONA 3a. ¡Mamá . . .!

MADRE. Es la verdad, hija mía. No nos podemos extralimitar lo más mínimo. Muchas veces les pregunto: «¿Qué queréis, hijas de mi alma: huevo en el almuerzo o silla en el paseo?». Y ellas me responden las tres a la vez: «Sillas».

SOLTERONA 3ª. Mamá, no comentes más esto. Todo Granada lo sabe.

FIRST SPINSTER. Hardly any.

MOTHER. My favourite's the syringa.

THIRD SPINSTER. And violets are quite wonderful!

Pause.

MOTHER. Well, my dears, what about the card?

THIRD SPINSTER. Of course. It's a little girl dressed in pink, and she acts as a barometer. The monk with the hood is far too common now. The girl's skirts are made of extremely thin paper, and they open and close according to the weather.

ROSITA (*reads the message*).

'In the meadow one morning
The nightingales singing.
Their song proclaims
Rosita's a darling.'

You really shouldn't have!

AUNT. Such good taste!

MOTHER. I've never lacked taste. Only money!

FIRST SPINSTER. Oh, Mama!

SECOND SPINSTER. Oh, Mama!

THIRD SPINSTER. Oh, Mama!

MOTHER. My dears, I'm among friends here. No one can hear us. (*To the* AUNT.) You know how, since my poor husband passed away, I've performed miracles in order to manage on a pension. I can still hear my girls' father, generous soul that he was, telling me: 'Enriqueta, spend, spend! I'm earning decent money.' Alas, those days are gone. But, even so, we've managed to keep our position in society. What agonies I've gone through, madam, so my girls should not be deprived of hats! The tears I've shed on account of a ribbon or an arrangement of curls! Those feathers and wires have cost me many a sleepless night!

THIRD SPINSTER. Mama!

MOTHER. But it's the truth, my child. We can't afford to spend beyond our means. Many's the time I say to them: 'Tell me, dear girls, which would you really prefer: an egg for lunch or a seat at the evening promenade?' They all reply immediately: 'A seat, a seat!'

THIRD SPINSTER. Oh, Mama, don't go on! The whole of Granada's heard it!

MADRE. Claro, ¿qué van a contestar? Y allá nos vamos con
unas patatas y un racimo de uvas, pero con capa de mongolia
o sombrilla pintada o blusa de popelinette, con todos los
detalles. Porque no hay más remedio. ¡Pero a mí me cuesta la
vida! Y se me llenan los ojos de lágrimas cuando las veo
alternar con las que pueden.

SOLTERONA 2a. ¿No vas ahora a la Alameda, Rosita?

ROSITA. No.

SOLTERONA 3a. Allí nos reunimos siempre con las de Ponce
de León, con las de Herrasti y con las de la baronesa de
Santa Matilde de la Bendición Papal. Lo mejor de
Granada.

MADRE. ¡Claro! Estuvieron juntas en el Colegio de la Puerta del
Cielo.

Pausa.

TÍA (*levantándose*). Tomarán ustedes algo. (*Se levantan
todas.*)

MADRE. No hay manos como las de usted para el piñonate y el
pastel de gloria.

SOLTERONA 1a. (*a* ROSITA). ¿Tienes noticias?

ROSITA. El último correo me prometía novedades. Veremos a
ver éste.

SOLTERONA 3a. ¿Has terminado el juego de encajes
valenciennes?

ROSITA. ¡Toma! Ya he hecho otro de nansú con mariposas a la
aguada.

SOLTERONA 2a. El día que te cases vas a llevar el mejor ajuar
del mundo.

ROSITA. ¡Ay, yo pienso que todo es poco! Dicen que los
hombres se cansan de una si la ven siempre con el mismo
vestido.

AMA (*entrando*). Ahí están las de Ayola, el fotógrafo.

TÍA. Las señoritas de Ayola, querrás decir.

AMA. Ahí están las señoronas por todo lo alto de Ayola,
fotógrafo de Su Majestad y medalla de oro en la exposición
de Madrid. (*Sale.*)

TÍA. Hay que aguantarla; pero a veces me crispa los nervios.
(*Las* SOLTERONAS *están con* ROSITA *viendo unos paños.*)
Están imposibles.

MOTHER. But I ask you, what else would they say? We may
have to survive on potatoes and grapes, but at least we have
our Mongolian capes, our painted parasols, and our
poplinette blouses with all the trimmings. What alternative is
there? But it's such a strain! It makes me weep when I see
them mixing with girls who are much better off.

SECOND SPINSTER. Don't you promenade of an evening any
more, Rosita?

ROSITA. I've given it up.

THIRD SPINSTER. We always meet up with the Ponce de León
girls, or the Herrastis, or the daughters of the Baroness of Saint
Matilda of the Papal Benediction. The cream of Granada.

MOTHER. You see, they were all together at Heaven's Gate
School.

Pause.

AUNT (*getting up*). Will you have something to eat? (*They all
stand.*)

MOTHER. You have the most delicate touch when it comes to
candied pine-nuts and angel cakes.

FIRST SPINSTER (*to* ROSITA). Have you had any news?

ROSITA. The last letter suggested there might be soon. I'm
waiting to see what this one brings.

THIRD SPINSTER. Have you finished the set with Valencian
lace?

ROSITA. Of course! And another of nainsook with moiré
butterflies.

SECOND SPINSTER. When you get married, you'll have the best
trousseau in the entire world.

ROSITA. Oh, I doubt it's enough yet! They say that a man gets
bored with a girl if she's always dressed in the same clothes.

HOUSEKEEPER (*entering*). The Ayola sisters are here. The
photographer's girls!

AUNT. I think you mean the Señoritas Ayola!

HOUSEKEEPER. The esteemed daughters of the high and mighty
Ayola, photographer to His Majesty the King, winner of the
Gold Medal at the Madrid Exhibition! (*Exits.*)

AUNT. One has to put up with her, but sometimes she does get
on my nerves. (*The* SPINSTERS *and* ROSITA *are looking at
some material.*) Servants are quite impossible.

MADRE. Envalentonadas. Yo tengo una muchacha que nos arregla el piso por las tardes; ganaba lo que han ganado siempre: una peseta al mes y las sobras, que ya está bien en estos tiempos; pues el otro día se nos descolgó diciendo que quería un duro, ¡y yo no puedo!

TÍA. No sé dónde vamos a parar.

Entran las NIÑAS DE AYOLA, *que saludan a* ROSITA *con alegría. Vienen con la moda exageradísima de la época y ricamente vestidas.*

ROSITA. ¿No se conocen ustedes?

AYOLA 1a. De vista.

ROSITA. Las señoritas de Ayola, la señora y señoritas de Escarpini.

AYOLA 2a. Ya las vemos sentadas en sus sillas del paseo. (*Disimulan la risa.*)

ROSITA. Tomen asiento.

Se sientan las SOLTERONAS.

TÍA (*a las de* AYOLA). ¿Queréis un dulcecito?

AYOLA 2a. No; hemos comido hace poco. Por cierto que yo tomé cuatro huevos con picadillo de tomate, y casi no me podía levantar de la silla.

AYOLA 1a. ¡Qué graciosa! (*Ríen.*)

Pausa. Las AYOLA *inician una risa incontenible que se comunica a* ROSITA, *que hace esfuerzos por contenerse. Las* CURSILONAS *y su* MADRE *están serias. Pausa.*

TÍA. ¡Qué criaturas!

MADRE. ¡La juventud!

TÍA. Es la edad dichosa.

ROSITA (*andando por la escena como arreglando cosas*). Por favor, callarse. (*Se callan.*)

TÍA (*a la* SOLTERONA 3a). ¿Y ese piano?

SOLTERONA 3a. Ahora estudio poco. Tengo muchas labores que hacer.

ROSITA. Hace mucho tiempo que no te he oído.

MADRE. Si no fuera por mí, ya se le habrían engarabitado los

MOTHER. And so insolent! I have a girl who cleans the apartment in the afternoons. She was earning what they've always earned – a peseta a month and the leftovers. You'd think it sufficient in times like these, but suddenly she asks for five pesetas, which I can't possibly manage.

AUNT. I can't imagine where it's going to end.

The AYOLA GIRLS *enter. They greet* ROSITA *excitedly. They are expensively dressed in the exaggerated style of the period.*

ROSITA. Do you know each other?

FIRST AYOLA. Only by sight.

ROSITA. The Señoritas Ayola, Señora Escarpini and the Señoritas Escarpini.

SECOND AYOLA. We see them sitting when we promenade. (*They struggle not to laugh.*)

ROSITA. Do sit down.

The SPINSTERS *sit.*

AUNT (*to the* AYOLA GIRLS). Would you like a sweet?

SECOND AYOLA. Thank you, no. We've not long eaten. To tell you the truth, I had four eggs with chopped tomato. I could barely walk.

FIRST AYOLA. She's so amusing! (*They laugh.*)

Pause. The AYOLAS *begin to laugh uncontrollably. It communicates itself to* ROSITA, *who tries not to laugh. The* SPINSTERS *and the* MOTHER *are serious. Pause.*

AUNT. Such children!

MOTHER. What it is to be young!

AUNT. Such happy times!

ROSITA (*walking around the room, as if arranging things*). Oh, do be quiet! Please!

They stop laughing.

AUNT (*to the* THIRD SPINSTER). Why don't you play for us?

THIRD SPINSTER. Oh, I haven't practised for ages. There's so much needlework!

ROSITA. It's so long since I heard you play.

MOTHER. If it weren't for me, her fingers would have seized up.

dedos. Pero siempre estoy con el tole tole.

SOLTERONA 2a. Desde que murió el pobre papá no tiene ganas.
¡Como a él le gustaba tanto!

SOLTERONA 3a. Me acuerdo que algunas veces se le caían las
lágrimas.

SOLTERONA 1a. Cuando tocaba la tarantela de Popper.

SOLTERONA 2a. Y la plegaria de la Virgen.

MADRE. ¡Tenía mucho corazón!

Las AYOLA, *que han estado conteniendo la risa, rompen a
reír en grandes carcajadas.* ROSITA, *vuelta de espaldas a
las* SOLTERONAS, *ríe también, pero se domina.*

TÍA. ¡Qué chiquillas!

AYOLA 1a. Nos reímos porque antes de entrar aquí . . .

AYOLA 2a. Tropezó ésta y estuvo a punto de dar la vuelta de
campana . . .

AYOLA 1ª. Y yo . . . (*Ríen.*)

Las SOLTERONAS *inician una leve risa fingida con un
matiz cansado y triste.*

MADRE.¡Ya nos vamos!

TÍA. De ninguna manera.

ROSITA (*a todas*). ¡Pues celebremos que no te hayas caído!
Ama, trae los huesos de Santa Catalina.

SOLTERONA 3a. ¡Qué ricos son!

MADRE. El año pasado nos regalaron a nosotras medio kilo.

Entra el AMA *con los huesos.*

AMA. Bocados para gente fina. (*A* ROSITA.) Ya viene el correo
por los alamillos.

ROSITA. ¡Espéralo en la puerta!

AYOLA 1a. Yo no quiero comer. Prefiero una palomilla de anís.

AYOLA 2a. Y yo de agraz.

ROSITA. ¡Tú siempre tan borrachilla!

AYOLA 1a. Cuando yo tenía seis años venía aquí y el novio de
Rosita me acostumbró a beberlas. ¿No recuerdas, Rosita?

ROSITA (*seria*). ¡No!

AYOLA 2a. A mí Rosita y su novio me enseñaban las letras A,
B, C . . . ¿Cuánto tiempo hace de esto?

I'm always telling her: 'Practise, practise!'

SECOND SPINSTER. Since poor Papa died she's hardly played at all. He loved to listen.

THIRD SPINSTER. I remember the tears would run down his cheeks.

FIRST SPINSTER. Whenever she played Popper's 'Tarantella'.

SECOND SPINSTER. And 'The Virgin's Prayer'.

MOTHER. He was such a sensitive soul!

The AYOLAS, *who have been restraining themselves, burst out laughing. Great peals of laughter.* ROSITA, *with her back to the* SPINSTERS, *laughs too, but controls herself.*

AUNT. What children you are!

FIRST AYOLA. We are laughing because, before we got here . . .

SECOND AYOLA. She tripped and almost went head over heels.

FIRST AYOLA. And I . . .

They laugh and the SPINSTERS *pretend to laugh in a somewhat sad and weary manner.*

MOTHER. Well, we'd best be going.

AUNT. Oh, no. You can't go yet.

ROSITA (*to everyone*). We'll celebrate the fact you didn't hurt yourself. (*To the* HOUSEKEEPER.) Bring the Saint Catherine's Bones.

THIRD SPINSTER. Oh, they are so delicious!

MOTHER. Last year someone gave us a whole half kilo.

The HOUSEKEEPER *enters with the 'bones'.*

HOUSEKEEPER. Titbits for fine people! (*To* ROSITA.) The postman's coming through the poplar trees.

ROSITA. Wait for him at the door.

FIRST AYOLA. I'm not really hungry. I'd much prefer some anisette.

SECOND AYOLA. Could I have some grape juice?

ROSITA. You were always fond of a tipple!

FIRST AYOLA. I used to call here when I was six. Rosita's fiancé got me used to it. Don't you remember, Rosita?

ROSITA (*seriously*). I don't think so, no.

SECOND AYOLA. Rosita and her fiancé used to teach me my ABC. How many years ago?

TÍA. ¡Quince años!

AYOLA 1a. A mí, casi, casi, se me ha olvidado la cara de tu novio.

AYOLA 2a. ¿No tenía una cicatriz en el labio?

ROSITA. ¿Una cicatriz? Tía, ¿tenía una cicatriz?

TÍA. Pero ¿no te acuerdas, hija? Era lo único que le afeaba un poco.

ROSITA. Pero no era una cicatriz; era una quemadura, un poquito rosada. Las cicatrices son hondas.

AYOLA 1a. ¡Tengo una gana de que Rosita se case!

ROSITA. ¡Por Dios!

AYOLA 2a. Nada de tonterías. ¡Yo también!

ROSITA. ¿Por qué?

AYOLA 1ª. Para ir a una boda. En cuanto yo pueda, me caso.

TÍA ¡Niña!

AYOLA 1a. Con quien sea, pero no me quiero quedar soltera.

AYOLA 2a. Yo pienso igual.

TÍA (*a la* Madre). ¿Qué le parece a usted?

AYOLA 1a. ¡Ay! ¡Y si soy amiga de Rosita es porque sé que tiene novio! Las mujeres sin novio están pochas, recocidas y todas ellas . . . (*Al ver a las* SOLTERONAS.) Bueno, todas, no; algunas de ellas . . . En fin, ¡todas están rabiadas!

TÍA. ¡Ea! Ya está bien.

MADRE. Déjela.

SOLTERONA 1a. Hay muchas que no se casan porque no quieren.

AYOLA 2a. Eso no lo creo yo.

SOLTERONA 1a (*con intención*). Lo sé muy cierto.

AYOLA 2a. La que no se quiere casar deja de echarse polvos y ponerse postizos debajo de la pechera, y no se está día y noche en las barandillas del balcón atisbando la gente.

SOLTERONA 2a. ¡Le puede gustar tomar el aire!

ROSITA. Pero ¡qué discusión más tonta! (*Ríen forzadamente.*)

TÍA. Bueno. ¿Por qué no tocamos un poquito?

MADRE. ¡Anda, niña!

SOLTERONA 3a. (*levantándose.*) Pero ¿qué toco?

AYOLA 2a. Toca ¡«Viva Frascuelo»!

AUNT. Fifteen!

FIRST AYOLA. I've almost forgotten what your fiancé looked like.

SECOND AYOLA. Didn't he have a scar on his lip?

ROSITA. A scar? Did he, Aunt?

AUNT. Don't you remember, child? It was the one thing that spoilt his face.

ROSITA. But it wasn't a scar. It was more like a burn, a red mark. Scars are much deeper.

FIRST AYOLA. I do hope Rosita gets married!

ROSITA. For heaven's sake!

SECOND AYOLA. Oh, come along! So do I!

ROSITA. But why?

FIRST AYOLA. So we can come to the wedding! I intend getting married as soon as I can.

AUNT. Really!

FIRST AYOLA. I don't mind who to. I'd rather not be left on the shelf!

SECOND AYOLA. And so say I!

AUNT (*to the* MOTHER). What's your opinion?

FIRST AYOLA. I'm Rosita's friend because she has a sweetheart. Girls without one are faded, dried-up creatures, all of them . . . (*Glancing at the* SPINSTERS.) well, some at least . . . boiling up inside!

AUNT. That's quite enough!

MOTHER. Pay no attention!

FIRST SPINSTER. Some girls don't get married because they don't wish to.

SECOND AYOLA. I don't believe a word of it.

FIRST SPINSTER (*meaningfully*). I know it for a fact!

SECOND AYOLA. A girl who doesn't want to get married doesn't powder her face or pad our her chest. And she doesn't sit on her balcony eyeing all the passers-by!

SECOND SPINSTER. Perhaps such a girl enjoys fresh air.

ROSITA. Oh, what a ridiculous conversation!

They all laugh in a forced manner.

AUNT. Why don't we have some music?

MOTHER. Yes. Come along, child!

THIRD SPINSTER (*getting up*). What shall I play?

SOLTERONA 2a. La barcarola de «La fragata Numancia».

ROSITA. ¿Y por qué no «Lo que dicen las flores»?

MADRE. ¡Ah, sí, «Lo que dicen las flores»! (*A la* TÍA.) ¿No la ha oído usted? Habla y toca al mismo tiempo. ¡Una preciosidad!

SOLTERONA 3a. También puedo decir «Volverán las oscuras golondrinas de tu balcón los nidos a colgar».

AYOLA 1a. Eso es muy triste.

SOLTERONA 1a. Lo triste es bonito también.

TÍA. ¡Vamos! ¡Vamos!

SOLTERONA 3a (*en el piano*).
Madre, llévame a los campos
con la luz de la mañana
a ver abrirse las flores
cuando se mecen las ramas.
Mil flores dicen mil cosas
para mil enamoradas,
y la fuente está contando
lo que el ruiseñor se calla.

ROSITA.
Abierta estaba la rosa
con la luz de la mañana;
tan roja de sangre tierna,
que el rocío se alejaba;
tan caliente sobre el tallo,
que la brisa se quemaba;
¡tan alta!, ¡cómo reluce!
¡Abierta estaba!

SOLTERONA 3a.
«Sólo en ti pongo mis ojos»,
el heliotropo expresaba.
«No te querré mientras viva»,
dice la flor de la albahaca.
«Soy tímida», la violeta.
«Soy fría», la rosa blanca.
Dice el jazmín: «Seré fiel»;
y el clavel: «¡Apasionada!»

SOLTERONA 2a.
El jacinto es la amargura;
el dolor, la pasionaria.

SECOND AYOLA. What about 'Viva Frascuelo!'?

SECOND SPINSTER. The barcarole from 'The Frigate *Numancia*'.

ROSITA. I'd like to hear 'What the Flowers Say'.

MOTHER. Yes, yes! 'What the Flowers Say'! (*To the* AUNT.)
Have you heard her? She recites and plays at the same time.
It's absolute perfection.

THIRD SPINSTER. I could also do 'The dark swallows will soon
return, to build their nests on your balcony'.

FIRST AYOLA. Oh, no! That's terribly sad.

FIRST SPINSTER. But sad things can be beautiful.

AUNT. Oh, come along now! Come along!

THIRD SPINSTER (*at the piano*).

Mother, take me to the fields
As day begins to break,
To see the flowers open
And the branches start to wake.
A thousand flowers whisper to
A thousand love-struck maidens;
The fountain tells a story
Which the nightingale keeps hidden.

ROSITA.

The rose has opened quickly
In the early morning light;
As red as blood that's newly spilled,
It puts the dew to flight.
So dazzling upon its stem,
Its fire burns the air;
How tall it stands, how splendid!
Its petals bright and fair.

THIRD SPINSTER.

'Only on you do I set my eyes,'
The heliotrope would sigh.
'And I can never love you,'
Is the basil-flower's cry.
The violet says: 'I'm timid';
The white rose says: 'I'm cold';
The jasmine says: 'I'm faithful';
The carnation boasts: 'I'm bold'.

SECOND SPINSTER.

The hyacinth means bitterness,
The passion-flower pain.

SOLTERONA 1a.
> El jaramago, el desprecio,
> y los lirios, la esperanza.

TÍA.
> Dice el nardo: «Soy tu amigo»;
> «creo en ti», la pasionaria.
> La madreselva te mece,
> la siempreviva te mata.

MADRE.
> Siempreviva de la muerte,
> flor de las manos cruzadas,
> ¡qué bien estás cuando el aire
> llora sobre tu guirnalda!

ROSITA.
> Abierta estaba la rosa,
> pero la tarde llegaba,
> y un rumor de nieve triste
> le fue pasando las ramas;
> cuando la sombra volvía,
> cuando el ruiseñor cantaba,
> como una muerta de pena
> se puso transida y blanca;
> y cuando la noche, grande
> cuerno de metal sonaba
> y los vientos enlazados
> dormían en la montaña,
> se deshojó suspirando
> por los cristales del alba.

SOLTERONA 3a.
> Sobre tu largo cabello
> gimen las flores cortadas.
> Unas llevan puñalitos;
> otras, fuego, y otras, agua.

SOLTERONA 1a.
> Las flores tienen su lengua
> para las enamoradas.

ROSITA.
> Son celos el carambuco;
> desdén esquivo, la dalia;

FIRST SPINSTER.

The lily is eternal hope,
The mustard-flower disdain.

AUNT.

The spike-nard says: 'I am your friend';
The passion-flower: 'I trust you';
The honeysuckle soothes,
But the immortelle will kill you.

MOTHER.

The immortelle that stands for death,
Clasped tight by hands that pray;
How fine you seem when the gentle breeze
Weeps on a funeral day.

ROSITA.

The rose's petals open wide
As evening advances;
And the sad sound of falling snow,
Heavy on the branches.
When shadows fall and nightingales sing,
Recounting their sad tale,
Like someone overwhelmed by grief,
The rose grows white and pale.
When night arrives, announcing itself
On its great metallic horn,
When the winds, asleep on the mountain top,
Have long since ceased to moan;
Then it is that her death begins
And she longs in vain for the dawn.

THIRD SPINSTER.

Dead flowers weep in your long hair,
Some are as sharp as knives;
And others are water or fire,
Matching a young girl's sighs.

FIRST SPINSTER.

The flowers have a language,
A meaning of their own.
Who can understand it?
Those by love overthrown.

ROSITA.

The willow-herb speaks of jealousy,
The dahlia of disdain,

suspiros de amor, el nardo;
risa, la gala de Francia.
Las amarillas son odio;
el furor, las encarnadas;
las blancas son casamiento,
y las azules, mortaja.

SOLTERONA 3a.
Madre, llévame a los campos
con la luz de la mañana,
a ver abrirse las flores
cuando se mecen las ramas.

El piano hace la última escala y se para.

TÍA. ¡Ay, qué preciosidad!

MADRE. Saben también el lenguaje del abanico, el lenguaje de los guantes, el lenguaje de los sellos y el lenguaje de las horas. A mí se me pone la carne de gallina cuando dicen aquello:

Las doce dan sobre el mundo
con horrísono rigor;
de la hora de tu muerte
acuérdate, pecador.

AYOLA 1a. (*con la boca llena de dulce*). ¡Qué cosa más fea!

MADRE.
Y cuando dicen:

A la una nacemos,
la ra la, la,
y este nacer,
la, la, ran,
es como abrir los ojos,
lan,
en un vergel,
vergel, vergel.

AYOLA 2a. (*a su* HERMANA). Me parece que la vieja ha empinado el codo. (*A la* MADRE.) ¿Quiere otra copita?

MADRE. Con sumo gusto y fina voluntad, como se decía en mi época.

ROSITA *ha estado esperando la llegada del correo.*

AMA. ¡El correo!

The fleur-de-lys of laughter,
The spike-nard of love's pain.
Yellow flowers all mean hate,
Scarlet passion's heat,
White foretells a bridal gown,
Blue a fatal winding-sheet.

THIRD SPINSTER.

Mother, take me to the fields
As day begins to break,
To see the flowers open
And the branches start to wake.

(*A final flourish on the piano.*)

AUNT. That was quite delightful!

MOTHER. They can also perform 'The Language of the Fan', 'The Gloves', 'Stamps', and 'The Hours'. I get goose-pimples when they get to the bit that goes:

The clock strikes twelve throughout the world,
Its sound is harsh and clear.
Let sinners ponder on their sins,
The hour of death draws near!

FIRST AYOLA (*her mouth full of sweets*). Oh, that's really hideous!

MOTHER. The same thing happens with:

At one o'clock we are born,
Tra, la, la.
To be born at such an hour,
Tra, la, la.
Is to open these eyes of ours,
Tra, la, la,
To a garden of lovely flowers,
Tra, la, la.

SECOND AYOLA (*to her sister*). I think the old girl's had a drop too much. (*To the* MOTHER.) Would you care for another glass?

MOTHER. I don't mind if I do. With the utmost pleasure and the best will in the world, as they used to say in my day.

ROSITA *has been looking out for the postman.*

HOUSEKEEPER. The post!

Algazara general.

TÍA. Y ha llegado justo.

SOLTERONA 3a. Ha tenido que contar los días para que llegue hoy.

MADRE. ¡Es una fineza!

AYOLA 2a. ¡Abre la carta!

AYOLA 1a. Más discreto es que la leas tú sola, porque a lo mejor te dice algo verde.

MADRE. ¡Jesús!

Sale ROSITA *con la carta.*

AYOLA 1a. Una carta de un novio no es un devocionario.

SOLTERONA 3a. Es un devocionario de amor.

AYOLA 2a. ¡Ay, qué finoda! (*Ríen las* AYOLA.)

AYOLA 1a. Se conoce que no ha recibido ninguna.

MADRE (*fuerte*). ¡Afortunadamente para ella!

AYOLA 1a. Con su pan se lo coma.

TÍA (*al* AMA, *que va a entrar con* ROSITA). ¿Dónde vas tú?

AMA. ¿Es que no puedo dar un paso?

TÍA. ¡Déjala a ella!

ROSITA (*saliendo*). ¡Tía! ¡Tía!

TÍA. Hija, ¿qué pasa?

ROSITA (*con agitación*). ¡Ay, tía!

AYOLA 1a. ¿Qué?

SOLTERONA 3a. ¡Dinos!

AYOLA 2a. ¿Qué?

AMA. ¡Habla!

TÍA. ¡Rompe!

MADRE. ¡Un vaso de agua!

AYOLA 2a. ¡Venga!

AYOLA 1a. Pronto.

Algazara.

ROSITA (*con voz ahogada*). Que se casa . . . (*Espanto en todos.*) Que se casa conmigo, porque ya no puede más, pero que . . .

AYOLA 2a. (*abrazándola*). ¡Olé! ¡Qué alegría!

AYOLA 1a. ¡Un abrazo!

General excitement.

AUNT. It couldn't be better timed!

THIRD SPINSTER. He must have meant it to arrive today.

MOTHER. How considerate of him!

SECOND AYOLA. Open it!

FIRST AYOLA. You'd better read it alone. He might have written something rather daring.

AUNT. For goodness' sake!

ROSITA *goes out with the letter.*

FIRST AYOLA. A love letter isn't a prayer book, you know.

THIRD SPINSTER. Oh, yes it is! It's a prayer book of love.

SECOND AYOLA. Oh, isn't that exquisite? (*The* AYOLAS *laugh.*)

FIRST AYOLA. It's obvious she's never received one.

MOTHER (*sternly*). And a good thing she hasn't!

FIRST AYOLA. Her problem, then!

AUNT (*to the* HOUSEKEEPER, *who is starting to go out to* ROSITA). Where are you going?

HOUSEKEEPER. Aren't I allowed to put one foot in front of the other?

AUNT. Just leave her be!

ROSITA (*entering*). Aunt, Aunt!

AUNT. What is it, child?

ROSITA (*excitedly*). Oh, Aunt!

FIRST AYOLA. What is it?

THIRD SPINSTER. Tell us!

SECOND AYOLA. What is it?

HOUSEKEEPER. Speak!

AUNT. Out with it!

MOTHER. A glass of water!

SECOND AYOLA. Tell us, tell us!

FIRST AYOLA. Spit it out!

Flurry of excitement.

ROSITA (*in a choking voice*). He's getting married . . . (*Alarm on all sides.*) He's going to marry *me*, because he can't bear to wait any more, but . . .

SECOND AYOLA (*hugging her*). Hooray! We're all so happy for you!

FIRST AYOLA. Give me a hug!

TÍA. Dejadla hablar.

ROSITA (*más calmada*). Pero como le es imposible venir por ahora, la boda será por poderes y luego vendrá él.

SOLTERONA 1a. ¡Enhorabuena!

MADRE (*casi llorando*). ¡Dios te haga lo feliz que mereces! (*La abraza.*)

AMA. Bueno, y «poderes» ¿qué es?

ROSITA. Nada. Una persona representa al novio en la ceremonia.

AMA. ¿Y qué más?

ROSITA. ¡Que está una casada!

AMA. Y por la noche, ¿qué?

ROSITA. ¡Por Dios!

AYOLA 1a. Muy bien dicho. Y por la noche, ¿qué?

TÍA. ¡Niñas!

AMA. ¡Que venga en persona y se case! ¡«Poderes»! No lo he oído decir nunca. La cama y sus pinturas temblando de frío, y la camisa de novia en lo más oscuro del baúl. Señora, no deje usted que los «poderes» entren en esta casa. (*Ríen todos.*) ¡Señora, que yo no quiero «poderes»!

ROSITA. Pero él vendrá pronto. ¡Esto es una prueba más de lo que me quiere!

AMA. ¡Eso! ¡Que venga y que te coja del brazo y que menee el azúcar de tu café y lo pruebe antes a ver si quema! (*Risas.*)

Aparece el TÍO *con una rosa.*

ROSITA. ¡Tío!

TÍO. Lo he oído todo, y casi sin darme cuenta he cortado la única rosa mudable que tenía en mi invernadero. Todavía estaba roja:

Abierta en el mediodía,
es roja como el coral.

ROSITA.

El sol se asoma a los vidrios
para verla relumbrar.

TÍO. Si hubiera tardado dos horas más en cortarla te la hubiese dado blanca.

ROSITA.

Blanca como la paloma,
como la risa del mar;

AUNT. Let her speak!

ROSITA (*more calmly*). But at the moment he can't come, so the wedding will be by proxy, and he'll be coming later.

FIRST SPINSTER. Congratulations!

MOTHER (*almost weeping*). May God grant you the happiness you deserve! (*She embraces* ROSITA).

HOUSEKEEPER. So what's this 'by proxy'? What's it mean?

ROSITA. It means that someone stands in for the groom at the wedding.

HOUSEKEEPER. What else?

ROSITA. And then I'm married.

HOUSEKEEPER. So what about the nights?

ROSITA. For goodness' sake!

FIRST AYOLA. A good point! What about the nights?

AUNT. Girls! Really!

HOUSEKEEPER. Let him come himself and marry you! 'By proxy', indeed! I've never heard of it. The bedsheets and covers trembling with cold and the bride's nightdress still in the drawer! Señora, never let 'proxies' into this house! (*They all laugh.*) I'll have nothing to do with 'proxies'.

ROSITA. But he'll soon be here in person. It's proof of how much he loves me!

HOUSEKEEPER. Good! Let him come and take you by the arm. Let him stir the sugar in your coffee and taste it first to see if it's too hot!

Laughter. The UNCLE *enters with a rose.*

ROSITA. Uncle!

UNCLE. I heard everything and, without thinking, cut the only mutable rose I had. It was still red:

By noon her petals, open wide,
Have all the firmness of coral.

ROSITA.
The jealous sun looks down upon
The splendour of its rival.

UNCLE. If I'd waited two hours more, it would have been white.

ROSITA.
Like the whiteness of a dove,
Like the sea's sad smiling,

blanca como el blanco frío
de una mejilla de sal.

TÍO. Pero todavía, todavía tiene la brasa de su juventud.

TÍA. Bebe conmigo una copita, hombre. Hoy es día de que lo
hagas.

> *Algazara. La* SOLTERONA *3a se sienta al piano y toca una
> polca.* ROSITA *está mirando la rosa. Las* SOLTERONAS *2a
> y 1a bailan con las* AYOLA *y cantan.*

Porque mujer te vi
a la orilla del mar,
tu dulce languidez
me hacía suspirar,
y aquel dulzor sutil
de mi ilusión fatal
a la luz de la luna
lo viste naufragar.

> *La* TÍA *y el* TÍO *bailan.* ROSITA *se dirige a la pareja*
> SOLTERA *2a. y* AYOLA. *Baila con la* SOLTERA. *La* AYOLA
> *bate palmas al ver a los viejos y el* AMA *al entrar hace el
> mismo juego.*

Telón.

Like the pale white coldness
Of a cheek marked by grieving.

UNCLE. But for now it has the fire of youth.
AUNT. Husband! We shall drink to it. A day to celebrate!

> *Excitement. The* THIRD SPINSTER *goes to the piano and plays a polka.* ROSITA *is looking at the rose. The* FIRST *and* SECOND SPINSTERS *dance with the* AYOLAS *and sing:*

I saw you, young woman,
On the seashore standing.
Your sweet, sad manner
Was the cause of my longing.
That delicate sweetness
Of my fatal illusion,
In the light of the moon
Was sudden confusion.

> *The* AUNT *and* UNCLE *dance.* ROSITA *goes to the couple formed by the* SECOND SPINSTER *and the* AYOLA. *She dances with the* SPINSTER. *On seeing the old couple dance, the* AYOLA *claps her hands. The* HOUSEKEEPER *enters and joins in.*

> *Curtain.*

Acto tercero

Sala baja de ventanas con persianas verdes que dan al jardín del carmen. Hay un silencio en la escena. Un reloj da las seis de la tarde. Cruza la escena el AMA con un cajón y una maleta. Han pasado diez años. Aparece la TÍA y se sienta en una silla baja, en el centro de la escena. Silencio.

El reloj vuelve a dar las seis. Pausa.

AMA (*entrando*). La repetición de las seis.

TÍA. ¿Y la niña?

AMA. Arriba, en la torre. Y usted, ¿dónde estaba?

TÍA. Quitando las últimas macetas del invernadero.

AMA. No la he visto en toda la mañana.

TÍA. Desde que murió mi marido está la casa tan vacía que parece el doble de grande, y hasta tenemos que buscarnos. Algunas noches, cuando toso en mi cuarto, oigo un eco como si estuviera en una iglesia.

AMA. Es verdad que la casa resulta demasiado grande.

TÍA. Y luego . . ., si él viviera, con aquella claridad que tenía, con aquel talento . . . (*Casi llorando.*)

AMA (*cantando*). Lan-lan-van-lan-lan . . . No, señora, llorar no lo consiento. Hace ya seis años que murió y no quiero que esté usted como el primer día. ¡Bastante lo hemos llorado! ¡A pisar firme, señora! ¡Salga el sol por las esquinas! ¡Que nos espere muchos años todavía cortando rosas!

TÍA (*levantándose*). Estoy muy viejecita, ama. Tenemos encima una ruina muy grande.

AMA. No nos faltará. ¡También yo estoy vieja!

TÍA. ¡Ojalá tuviera yo tus años!

AMA. Nos llevamos poco, pero como yo he trabajado mucho, estoy engrasada, y a usted, a fuerza de poltrona, se le han engarabitado las piernas.

TÍA. ¿Es que te parece que yo no he trabajado?

AMA. Con las puntillas de los dedos, con hilos, con tallos, con confituras; en cambio, yo he trabajado con las espaldas, con las rodillas, con las uñas.

Act Three

A small sitting room with green-shuttered windows opening onto the garden. The stage is silent. A clock strikes six in the evening. The HOUSEKEEPER *crosses the stage carrying a box and a suitcase. Ten years have passed. The* AUNT *appears and sits on a low chair centre stage. Silence.*
The clock strikes six again. Pause.

HOUSEKEEPER (*entering*). Six o'clock for the second time.

AUNT. Where's our little girl?

HOUSEKEEPER. Up in the attic. Where were you?

AUNT. Moving the last few flowerpots out of the greenhouse.

HOUSEKEEPER. I haven't seen you all morning.

AUNT. Since my husband died, the house seems empty . . . and twice as big. It's as if we have to go looking for each other. When I cough in my room at night, I can hear it echoing as if I were in a church.

HOUSEKEEPER. The house is far too big, you're right.

AUNT. If only he were still here! He had such clarity of purpose, such talent . . . (*Almost weeping.*)

HOUSEKEEPER (*singing*). La la tra la la la la la . . . No, señora, you are not to cry. It's six years since he passed away, and I don't want to see you as you were then. We've cried enough for him! Our best foot forward, señora! Let the sun shine in the darkest corners! He can wait for us for a long time yet . . . busy himself up there with his roses!

AUNT (*rising*). I feel so old. Everything is such a burden.

HOUSEKEEPER. Oh, everything will be all right. I'm old too, you know.

AUNT. If only I were your age!

HOUSEKEEPER. There's not that much between us, but I've worked harder than you, so my joints are well oiled. Your legs have gone stiff from too much sitting around.

AUNT. You aren't suggesting I haven't worked?

HOUSEKEEPER. But you've only used your fingertips – sewing, pruning, making jam. I've worked with my back, with my knees, with my fingernails.

TÍA. Entonces, gobernar una casa ¿no es trabajar?

AMA. Es mucho más difícil fregar sus suelos.

TÍA. No quiero discutir.

AMA. ¿Y por qué no? Así pasamos el rato. Ande. Replíqueme.
Pero nos hemos quedado mudas. Antes se daban voces. Que
si esto, que si lo otro, que si las natillas, que si no planches
más . . .

TÍA. Yo ya estoy entregada . . ., y un día sopas, otro día
migas, mi vasito de agua y mi rosario en el bolsillo,
esperaría la muerte con dignidad . . . ¡Pero cuando pienso en
Rosita!

AMA. ¡Ésa es la llaga!

TÍA (*enardecida*). Cuando pienso en la mala acción que le han
hecho y en el terrible engaño mantenido y en la falsedad del
corazón de ese hombre, que no es de mi familia ni merece ser
de mi familia, quisiera tener veinte años para tomar un vapor
y llegar a Tucumán y coger un látigo . . .

AMA (*interrumpiéndola*). . . . y coger una espada y cortarle la
cabeza y machacársela con dos piedras y cortarle la mano del
falso juramento y las mentirosas escrituras de cariño.

TÍA. Sí, sí; que pagara con sangre lo que sangre ha costado,
aunque toda sea sangre mía, y después . . .

AMA. . . . aventar las cenizas sobre el mar.

TÍA. Resucitarlo y traerlo con Rosita para respirar satisfecha
con la honra de los míos.

AMA. Ahora me dará usted la razón.

TÍA. Te la doy.

AMA. Allí encontró la rica que iba buscando y se casó, pero
debió decirlo a tiempo. Porque ¿quién quiere ya a esta
mujer? ¡Ya está pasada! Señora, ¿y no le podríamos mandar
una carta envenenada, que se muriera de repente al
recibirla?

TÍA. ¡Qué cosas! Ocho años lleva de matrimonio, y hasta el mes
pasado no me escribió el canalla la verdad. Yo notaba algo
en las cartas; los poderes que no venían, un aire dudoso . . .,
no se atrevía, pero al fin lo hizo. ¡Claro que después que su
padre murió! Y esta criatura . . .

AMA. ¡Chist . . .!

TÍA. Y recoge las dos orzas.

AUNT. You think that running a house isn't work?

HOUSEKEEPER. It's much harder scrubbing the floors.

AUNT. I don't want to argue.

HOUSEKEEPER. Why not? It helps to pass the time. Come on, answer me back! We've lost the use of our tongues. In the old days we used to raise our voices: 'What about this?'; 'You haven't done that!'; 'Where's the custard?'; 'Finish the ironing!'.

AUNT. I've had enough . . . all I want now is my bowl of soup, my bit of bread, my glass of water, my rosary in my pocket . . . I could die quite happily . . . But the thought of Rosita!

HOUSEKEEPER. That's what hurts!

AUNT. When I think of the wrong that's been done to her, of all the time she's been deceived, of the wickedness of that man's heart! He's not good enough to be one of my family! If I were twenty years of age, I'd take a boat to Tucumán and flay him alive . . .

HOUSEKEEPER (*breaking in*). . . . and cut off his head with a sword, and crush it between two stones, and chop off the hand that made false promises and wrote those love letters full of lies!

AUNT. He should be made to pay with blood for what has cost us blood, even if it were all my blood! And then . . .

HOUSEKEEPER. . . . scatter his ashes across the sea!

AUNT. Bring him to life again and give him to Rosita! Then I could breathe, knowing my family honour has been restored.

HOUSEKEEPER. You have to admit I was right.

AUNT. You were.

HOUSEKEEPER. When he found the rich girl he was looking for, he should have said so! Who's going to want Rosita now? She's far too old. Oh, señora, we could send him a poisoned letter! It would kill him as soon as he opened it!

AUNT. Can you believe it! He's been married for eight years, and the wretch only told us the truth a month ago. I could tell there was something wrong . . . the power of attorney that never came, all that hesitation . . . He didn't dare tell us . . . not until his father died! And this poor girl!

HOUSEKEEPER. There, there!

AUNT (*changing the subject*). And don't forget the two jars.

Aparece ROSITA. *Viene vestida de un rosa claro con moda del 1910. Entra peinada de bucles. Está muy avejentada.*

AMA. ¡Niña!

ROSITA. ¿Qué hacéis?

AMA. Criticando un poquito. Y tú, ¿dónde vas?

ROSITA. Voy al invernadero. ¿Se llevaron ya las macetas?

TÍA. Quedan unas pocas.

Sale ROSITA. *Se limpian las lágrimas las dos mujeres.*

AMA. ¿Y ya está? ¿Usted sentada y yo sentada? ¿Y a morir tocan? ¿Y no hay ley? ¿Y no hay gábilos para hacerlo polvo . . .?

TÍA. Calla, ¡no sigas!

AMA. Yo no tengo genio para aguantar estas cosas sin que el corazón me corra por todo el pecho como si fuera un perro perseguido. Cuando yo enterré a mi marido lo sentí mucho, pero tenía en el fondo una gran alegría . . .; alegría no . . ., golpetazos de ver que la enterrada no era yo. Cuando enterré a mi niña . . . ¿me entiende usted?, cuando enterré a mi niña fue como si me pisotearan las entrañas, pero los muertos son muertos. Están muertos, vamos a llorar, se cierra la puerta, ¡y a vivir! Pero esto de mi Rosita es lo peor. Es querer y no encontrar el cuerpo; es llorar y no saber por quién se llora; es suspirar por alguien que uno sabe que no se merece los suspiros. Es una herida abierta que mana sin parar un hilito de sangre, y no hay nadie, nadie en el mundo, que traiga los algodones, las vendas o el precioso terrón de nieve.

TÍA. ¿Qué quieres que yo haga?

AMA. Que nos lleve el río.

TÍA. A la vejez todo se nos vuelve de espaldas.

AMA. Mientras yo tenga brazos nada le faltará.

TÍA (*pausa. Muy bajo, como con vergüenza*). Ama, ¡ya no puedo pagar tus mensualidades! Tendrás que abandonarnos.

AMA. ¡Huuy! ¡Qué airazo entra por las ventanas! ¡Huuy! . . . ¿O será que me estoy volviendo sorda? Pues . . . ¿y las ganas que me entran de cantar? ¡Como los niños que salen del colegio! (*Se oyen voces infantiles.*) ¿Lo oye usted, señora? Mi

ROSITA *enters. She wears a light pink dress in the style of 1910. Her hair is in ringlets. She looks much older.*

HOUSEKEEPER. Child!

ROSITA. What are you doing?

HOUSEKEEPER. Just having a bit of a moan. Where are you going?

ROSITA. To the greenhouse. Have they taken the pots?

AUNT. There are still a few left.

ROSITA *leaves. The two women wipe away their tears.*

HOUSEKEEPER. Is this all there is? You sitting there, me here? And both of us waiting to die? Isn't there a law? Has no one got the courage to pulverise him?

AUNT. Sshh! Let's leave it.

HOUSEKEEPER. But it's not in my nature to just sit back. My heart scampers around like a dog that's being chased. When I buried my husband, I was really upset, but deep down I was happy too . . . well, not happy exactly . . . but glad that it wasn't me who had died. When I buried my little girl – you'll know what I mean – when I buried her, it was just as if they were stamping on my insides. But in the end the dead are dead, we cry, the door closes, and we have to go on. But this with my Rosita is worse than anything. It's like loving a person you can't get through to; crying and not being sure who you are crying for; sighing for someone you know doesn't deserve your sighs. It's an open wound that never stops bleeding, and yet there's no one, no one at all to bring the cotton wool, the bandages, the precious piece of ice.

AUNT. What do you want me to do?

HOUSEKEEPER. We have to go with the flow.

AUNT. Everything turns its back on old age.

HOUSEKEEPER. While I've got my strength, you'll lack for nothing.

AUNT (*pause, quietly, as if ashamed*). Woman, I can't go on paying you every month. You'll have to leave us.

HOUSEKEEPER. Wheeee! Listen to that wind through the window! Wheeee! Or am I going deaf? I don't know why, but I feel like singing! Like the children coming out of school! (*Sound of children's voices.*) Can you hear them, señora? Oh,

señora, más señora que nunca. (*La abraza.*)

TÍA. Oye.

AMA. Voy a guisar. Una cazuela de jureles perfumada con hinojos.

TÍA. ¡Escucha!

AMA. ¡Y un monte nevado! Le voy a hacer un monte nevado con grageas de colores ...

TÍA. ¡Pero, mujer! ...

AMA (*a voces*). ¡Digo! ... ¡Si está aquí don Martín! Don Martín, ¡adelante! ¡Vamos! Entretenga un poco a la señora.

> Sale rápida. Entra DON MARTÍN. *Es un viejo con el pelo rojo. Lleva una muleta con la que sostiene una pierna encogida. Tipo noble, de gran dignidad, con un aire de tristeza definitiva.*

TÍA. ¡Dichosos los ojos!

MARTÍN. ¿Cuándo es la arrancada definitiva?

TÍA. Hoy.

MARTÍN. ¡Qué se le va a hacer!

TÍA. La nueva casa no es esto. Pero tiene buenas vistas y un patinillo con dos higueras donde se pueden tener flores.

MARTÍN. Más vale así. (*Se sientan.*)

TÍA. ¿Y usted?

MARTÍN. Mi vida de siempre. Vengo de explicar mi clase de Preceptiva. Un verdadero infierno. Era una lección preciosa: «Concepto y definición de la Harmonía», pero a los niños no les interesa nada. ¡Y qué niños! A mí, como me ven inútil, me respetan un poquito; alguna vez un alfiler que otro en el asiento, o un muñequito en la espalda, pero a mis compañeros les hacen cosas horribles. Son los niños de los ricos y, como pagan, no se les puede castigar. Así nos dice siempre el director. Ayer se empeñaron en que el pobre señor Canito, profesor nuevo de Geografía, llevaba corsé; porque tiene un cuerpo algo retrepado, y cuando estaba solo en el patio, se reunieron los grandullones y los internos, lo desnudaron de cintura para arriba, lo ataron a una de las columnas del corredor y le arrojaron desde el balcón un jarro de agua.

my señora, more than ever my señora! (*Hugging her.*)

AUNT. Listen to me.

HOUSEKEEPER. I'm going to do some cooking. Baked mackerel with fennel.

AUNT. You must listen to me!

HOUSEKEEPER. And a lovely meringue sprinkled with coloured sugar . . .

AUNT. Woman!

HOUSEKEEPER (*loudly*). I mean it! . . . Oh, look, it's Don Martín! Come in, come in, Don Martín! Entertain the señora for a while.

> The HOUSEKEEPER *leaves quickly.* DON MARTÍN *enters. He is an old man with red hair. He walks with a crutch because he has a bad leg. He is a dignified, aristocratic man, but has a marked air of sadness.*

AUNT. What a nice surprise!

DON MARTÍN. So when are you pulling up roots?

AUNT. Why, today.

DON MARTÍN. You are going then?

AUNT. The new house isn't as nice as this. But it does have quite a nice view, and a small patio with two fig trees. At least we can grow some flowers.

DON MARTÍN. Much more suitable! (*They sit.*)

AUNT. So, how are you?

DON MARTÍN. Oh, much the same as usual. I've just been giving my class on rhetoric. More or less like being in hell! An excellent talk: 'The Concept and Definition of Harmony'. But the children couldn't care less. What monsters they are! They know I'm disabled, of course, so they do show some respect – the odd drawing-pin on the seat of my chair, or a paper doll stuck on my back. But as for my colleagues, the most terrible things! The children of wealthy parents, you see, and because they pay we aren't allowed to punish them. The headmaster insists. Why, yesterday, they claimed that poor Mr Canito, the new geography teacher, must be wearing a corset, just because he's rather narrow-waisted. So when they found him alone in the playground, the bullies and the boarders combined forces, stripped him to the waist, tied him to a pillar in the corridor, and poured a jug of water on his head.

TÍA. ¡Pobre criatura!

MARTÍN. Todos los días entro temblando en el colegio esperando lo que van a hacerme, aunque, como digo, respetan algo mi desgracia. Hace un rato tenían un escándalo enorme, porque el señor Consuegra, que explica latín admirablemente, había encontrado un excremento de gato sobre su lista de clase.

TÍA. ¡Son el enemigo!

MARTÍN. Son los que pagan y vivimos con ellos. Y créame usted que los padres se ríen luego de las infamias, porque como somos los pasantes y no les vamos a examinar los hijos, nos consideran como hombres sin sentimiento, como a personas situadas en el último escalón de gente que lleva todavía corbata y cuello planchado.

TÍA. ¡Ay, don Martín! ¡Qué mundo este!

MARTÍN. ¡Qué mundo! Yo soñaba siempre ser poeta. Me dieron una flor natural y escribí un drama que nunca se pudo representar.

TÍA. *¿La hija del Jefté?*

MARTÍN. ¡Eso es!

TÍA. Rosita y yo lo hemos leído. Usted nos lo prestó. ¡Lo hemos leído cuatro o cinco veces!

MARTÍN (*con ansia*). ¿Y qué . . .?

TÍA. Me gustó mucho. Se lo he dicho siempre. Sobre todo cuando ella va a morir y se acuerda de su madre y la llama.

MARTÍN. Es fuerte, ¿verdad? Un drama verdadero. Un drama de contorno y de concepto. Nunca se pudo representar. (*Rompiendo a recitar*).

¡Oh madre excelsa! Torna tu mirada
a la que en vil sopor rendida yace;
¡recibe tú las fúlgidas preseas
y el hórrido estertor de mi combate!

¿Y es que esto está mal? ¿Y es que no suena bien de acento y de cesura este verso: «y el hórrido estertor de mi combate»?

TÍA. ¡Precioso! ¡Precioso!

MARTÍN. Y cuando Glucinio se va a encontrar con Isaías y levanta el tapiz de la tienda . . .

AMA (*interrumpiéndole*). Por aquí.

Entran dos OBREROS *vestidos con trajes de pana.*

AUNT. The poor man!

DON MARTÍN. Every day I arrive at school in an absolute state, wondering what lies in store for me, though, as I say, they do respect my disability. A few days back there was the most terrible fuss. Mr Consuegra, a most wonderful Latin teacher, found the register covered in cat-droppings.

AUNT. Really! How could they!

DON MARTÍN. They pay, so we have to put up with them. The parents simply laugh at such pranks because we are only assistants. I mean, we aren't the ones who mark the exams. They think we have no feelings. Of all white-collar workers, you see, they regard us as the lowest of the low.

AUNT. Don Martín! What a world this is!

DON MARTÍN. Indeed! I always wanted to be a poet. I was born with a natural talent. I once wrote a play. Unperformed, I'm afraid.

AUNT. *Jephthah's Daughter.*

DON MARTÍN. That was it.

AUNT. Rosita and I both read it. You lent it to us. We've read it four or five times.

DON MARTÍN (*eagerly*). And?

AUNT. Oh, it was very good. I've told you that often enough. I especially like the bit where the heroine is on the point of death, remembers her mother, and calls out to her.

DON MARTÍN. Ah, yes indeed! A powerful scene! A true drama, with shape and depth. Yet never performed! (*He recites.*)

'Oh, Mother unequalled! Turn your eyes on her
Who lies before you in wretched trance!
Receive unto yourself these shining jewels!
Observe the fatal horror of death's advance!'

Not bad at all, is it? A fine ring to it and the last line has an impressive caesura: 'Observe the fatal horror of death's advance!'

AUNT. Wonderful! Quite wonderful!

DON MARTÍN. And the part when Glucinius goes to meet Isaiah and opens the flap of his tent . . .

HOUSEKEEPER (*interrupting him*). Through here!

Two WORKMEN *enter, dressed in overalls.*

OBRERO 1o. Buenas tardes.

MARTÍN y TÍA (*juntos*). Buenas tardes.

AMA. ¡Ése es! (*Señala un diván grande que hay al fondo de la habitación.*)

> Los HOMBRES *lo sacan lentamente como si sacaran un ataúd. El* AMA *los sigue. Silencio. Se oyen dos campanadas mientras salen los hombres con el diván.*

MARTÍN. ¿Es la Novena de Santa Gertrudis la Magna?

TÍA. Sí, en San Antón.

MARTÍN. ¡Es muy difícil ser poeta! Después quise ser farmacéutico. Es una vida tranquila.

TÍA. Mi hermano, que en gloria esté, era farmacéutico.

MARTÍN. Pero no pude. Tenía que ayudar a mi madre y me hice profesor. Por eso envidiaba yo tanto a su marido. Él fue lo que quiso.

TÍA. ¡Y le costó la ruina!

MARTÍN. Sí, pero es peor esto mío.

TÍA. Pero usted sigue escribiendo.

MARTÍN. No sé por qué escribo, porque no tengo ilusión, pero sin embargo es lo único que me gusta. ¿Leyó usted mi cuento de ayer en el segundo número de *Mentalidad Granadina*?

TÍA. ¿«El cumpleaños de Matilde»? Sí, lo leímos; una preciosidad.

MARTÍN. ¿Verdad que sí? Ahí he querido renovarme haciendo una cosa de ambiente actual; ¡hasta hablo de un aeroplano! Verdad es que hay que modernizarse. Claro que lo que más me gusta a mí son mis sonetos.

TÍA. ¡A las nueve musas del Parnaso!

MARTÍN. A las diez, a las diez. ¿No se acuerda usted que nombré décima musa a Rosita?

AMA (*entrando*). Señora, ayúdeme usted a doblar esta sábana. (*Se ponen a doblarla entre las dos.*) ¡Don Martín con su pelito rojo! ¿Por qué no se casó, hombre de Dios? ¡No estaría tan solo en esta vida!

MARTÍN. ¡No me han querido!

AMA. Es que ya no hay gusto. ¡Con la manera de hablar tan preciosa que tiene usted!

TÍA. ¡A ver si lo vas a enamorar!

FIRST WORKMAN. Afternoon!

AUNT *and* DON MARTÍN. Good afternoon!

HOUSEKEEPER. This one!

> *She points to a large divan at the back of the room. The men take it out slowly as if they are carrying a coffin. The* HOUSEKEEPER *goes out after them. Silence. A church bell rings twice as the men leave.*

DON MARTÍN. Is it the novena of St Gertrude the Great?

AUNT. Yes, at St Anthony's.

DON MARTÍN. It's so difficult to be a poet. After that I wanted to be a chemist. A much more peaceful kind of life.

AUNT. My brother, God bless him, was a chemist.

DON MARTÍN. But it didn't work out. I had to support my mother, you know, so I became a teacher. That's why I envied your husband so much. He was what he wanted to be.

AUNT. And it ruined him.

DON MARTÍN. Perhaps it did, but my situation is even worse.

AUNT. You still write.

DON MARTÍN. I don't know why. I've no illusions. But it's the only thing I like doing. Did you read my short story? It appeared yesterday in the second issue of *The Granada Intellectual*?

AUNT. 'Matilda's Birthday'? Of course we read it. An absolute delight!

DON MARTÍN. You really think so? I was trying to write something more up-to-date, more modern. So I mentioned an aeroplane. You do have to keep abreast of things. Even so, my sonnets are my greatest pleasure.

AUNT. To the nine Muses of Parnassus!

DON MARTÍN. The ten, the ten! Don't you remember I made Rosita the tenth?

HOUSEKEEPER (*entering*). Señora, could you help me fold this sheet? (*The two of them begin to fold it.*) Don Martín, you little redhead! You should have got married. You wouldn't be so lonely now.

DON MARTÍN. No one ever loved me.

HOUSEKEEPER. Which just goes to prove there's no good taste in the world. Why, you've got such a lovely way of speaking.

AUNT. Be careful he doesn't fall for you!

MARTÍN. ¡Que pruebe!

AMA. Cuando él explica en la sala baja del colegio, yo voy a la carbonería para oírlo. «¿Qué es idea?» «La representación intelectual de una cosa o un objeto.» ¿No es así?

MARTÍN. ¡Mírenla! ¡Mírenla!

AMA. Ayer decía a voces: «No; ahí hay hipérbaton», y luego . . . «el epinicio» . . . A mí me gustaría entender, pero como no entiendo me dan ganas de reír, y el carbonero, que siempre está leyendo un libro que se llama *Las ruinas de Palmira*, me echa unas miradas como si fueran dos gatos rabiosos. Pero aunque me ría, como ignorante, comprendo que don Martín tiene mucho mérito.

MARTÍN. No se le da hoy mérito a la Retórica y Poética, ni a la cultura universitaria.

Sale el AMA *rápida con la sábana doblada.*

TÍA. ¡Qué le vamos a hacer! Ya nos queda poco tiempo en este teatro.

MARTÍN. Y hay que emplearlo en la bondad y en el sacrificio.

Se oyen voces.

TÍA. ¿Qué pasa?

AMA (*apareciendo*). Don Martín, que vaya usted al colegio, que los niños han roto con un clavo las cañerías y están todas las clases inundadas.

MARTÍN. Vamos allá. Soñé con el Parnaso y tengo que hacer de albañil y fontanero. Con tal de que no me empujen o resbale . . . (*El* AMA *ayuda a levantarse a* DON MARTÍN.)

Se oyen voces.

AMA. ¡Ya va . . .! ¡Un poco de calma! ¡A ver si el agua sube hasta que no quede un niño vivo!

MARTÍN (*saliendo*). ¡Bendito sea Dios!

TÍA. Pobre, ¡qué sino el suyo!

AMA. Mírese en ese espejo. Él mismo se plancha los cuellos y

DON MARTÍN. Oh, that would be the day!

HOUSEKEEPER. When he's teaching on the ground floor of the school, I go to the coalshed. I can hear him from there. 'What is meant by an idea?' 'An idea is the intellectual representation of a thing or an object.' Isn't that what you say?

DON MARTÍN. Listen to her! Listen to her!

HOUSEKEEPER. Yesterday he was calling out: 'No, this is an example of hyperbaton.' And then: 'This is an epinicion.' I wish I knew what it meant, but I haven't a clue, so I start to laugh, and the coalman looks at me daggers – just because he's reading this book called *The Ruins of Palmyra*. I only laugh because I'm so ignorant, and I know that Don Martín's so clever.

DON MARTÍN. Nowadays rhetoric and poetics count for nothing. They even dismiss a university education.

The HOUSEKEEPER *goes out quickly, carrying the folded sheet.*

AUNT. What's to be done? We shan't be walking this stage for very much longer.

DON MARTÍN. We must do our best through acts of kindness and sacrifice.

AUNT. What's that?

Shouts are heard.

HOUSEKEEPER (*entering*). Don Martín! The school at once! The children have put a nail through the waterpipes! All the classrooms are flooded!

DON MARTÍN. I'm on my way! I dreamt of Parnassus and end up as a builder and a plumber! Let's hope I don't slip and drown!

The HOUSEKEEPER *helps* DON MARTÍN *out of his chair. Voices are heard.*

HOUSEKEEPER. All right, all right! Keep calm! Let's hope the water rises and drowns all the little brats!

DON MARTÍN (*leaving*). Praise be to God!

AUNT. Poor man! What a fate!

HOUSEKEEPER. A lesson to us all. He irons his collars and darns

cose sus calcetines, y cuando estuvo enfermo, que le llevé las
natillas, tenía una cama con unas sábanas que tiznaban como
el carbón y unas paredes y un lavabillo . . ., ¡ay!

TÍA. ¡Y otros, tanto!

AMA. Por eso siempre diré: ¡Malditos, malditos sean los ricos!
¡No quede de ellos ni las uñas de las manos!

TÍA. ¡Déjalos!

AMA. Pero estoy segura que van al infierno de cabeza. ¿Dónde
cree usted que estará don Rafael Salé, explotador de los
pobres, que enterraron anteayer, Dios le haya perdonado,
con tanto cura y tanta monja y tanto gori-gori? ¡En el
infierno! Y él dirá: «¡Que tengo veinte millones de pesetas, no
me apretéis con las tenazas! ¡Os doy cuarenta mil duros si me
arrancáis estas brasas de los pies!»; pero los demonios,
tizonazo por aquí, tizonazo por allá, puntapié que te quiero,
bofetadas en la cara, hasta que la sangre se le convierta en
carbonilla.

TÍA. Todos los cristianos sabemos que ningún rico entra en el
reino de los cielos, pero a ver si por hablar de ese modo vas a
parar también al infierno de cabeza.

AMA. ¿Al infierno yo? Del primer empujón que le doy a la
caldera de Pedro Botero hago llegar el agua caliente a los
confines de la tierra. No, señora, no. Yo entro en el cielo a la
fuerza (*Dulce.*) Con usted. Cada una en una butaca de seda
celeste que se meza ella sola, y unos abanicos de raso grana.
En medio de las dos, en un columpio de jazmines y matas de
romero, Rosita meciéndose, y detrás su marido cubierto de
rosas, como salió en su caja de esta habitación; con la misma
sonrisa, con la misma frente blanca como si fuera de cristal,
y usted se mece así, y yo así, y Rosita así, y detrás el Señor
tirándonos rosas como si las tres fuéramos un paso de nácar
lleno de cirios y caireles.

TÍA. Y los pañuelos para las lágrimas que se queden aquí
abajo.

AMA. Eso, que se fastidien. Nosotras, ¡juerga celestial!

TÍA. ¡Porque ya no nos queda una sola dentro del corazón!

OBRERO 1o. Ustedes dirán.

AMA. Vengan. (*Entran. Desde la puerta.*) ¡Ánimo!

his socks himself. When he was ill, I took him some custard. The bedsheets were as black as coal, and as for the walls and the wash-basin . . . You've never seen the like.

AUNT. And other people are so well-off.

HOUSEKEEPER. That's why I'll always say: Damn the rich! Get rid of them all, down to the last fingernail!

AUNT. Oh, let them be!

HOUSEKEEPER. They'll all go to hell head first! Where do you think Don Rafael Salé's going, the one they buried two days ago? He exploited the poor all his life, and at his funeral all those prayers, all those priests, all those nuns, all that mumbo-jumbo! He's on his way to hell, of course! He'll be pleading with them: 'I've got twenty million pesetas, don't touch me with those tongs! Forty thousand duros to take these burning coals away from my feet!' But it won't stop those demons. A prod here, a poke there, a kick elsewhere. They'll smack his face till his blood turns to charcoal!

AUNT. We know as Christians that no rich man shall enter the kingdom of heaven. But you carry on like this, and it's you who'll be going to hell head first.

HOUSEKEEPER. Oh, no! Not me, señora! I'd give Old Nick's cauldron such a push, the water would scald the very ends of the earth. You see, señora, I'm going to force my way into heaven. (*Sweetly.*) With you. Each one of us in an armchair of sky-blue silk, rocking, cooling ourselves with fans of scarlet satin. And Rosita between us, on a swing of jasmine and sprigs of rosemary, moving gently; and behind her your husband, covered with roses, just as he was when he left this room in his coffin, his forehead as white as crystal. You will be rocking yourself like this, and Rosita like this, and behind us the good Lord will be throwing roses, as if the three of us were a float in the Holy Week procession, decorated with mother-of-pearl, candles and flounces.

AUNT. And handkerchiefs for drying tears will be left down here.

HOUSEKEEPER. They can do what they like down here! We'll be enjoying ourselves up there!

AUNT. Not a single tear left!

FIRST WORKMAN (*entering*). What's next, madam?

HOUSEKEEPER. Come with me. (*As they go out, she calls back.*) Take heart, señora!

TÍA. ¡Dios te bendiga! (*Se sienta lentamente.*)

Aparece ROSITA *con un paquete de cartas en la mano. Silencio.*

TÍA. ¿Se han llevado ya la cómoda?

ROSITA. En este momento. Su prima Esperanza mandó un niño por un destornillador.

TÍA. Estarán armando las camas para esta noche. Debimos irnos temprano y haber hecho las cosas a nuestro gusto. Mi prima habrá puesto los muebles de cualquier manera.

ROSITA. Pero yo prefiero salir de aquí con la calle a oscuras. Si me fuera posible apagaría el farol. De todos modos las vecinas estarán acechando. Con la mudanza ha estado todo el día la puerta llena de chiquillos, como si en la casa hubiera un muerto.

TÍA. Si yo lo hubiera sabido no hubiese consentido de ninguna manera que tu tío hubiera hipotecado la casa con muebles y todo. Lo que sacamos es lo sucinto, la silla para sentarnos y la cama para dormir.

ROSITA. Para morir.

TÍA. ¡Fue buena jugada la que nos hizo! ¡Mañana vienen los nuevos dueños! Me gustaría que tu tío nos viera. ¡Viejo tonto! Pusilánime para los negocios. ¡Chalado de las rosas! ¡Hombre sin idea del dinero! Me arruinaba cada día. «Ahí está Fulano»; y él: «Que entre»; y entraba con los bolsillos vacíos y salía con ellos rebosando plata, y siempre: «Que no se entere mi mujer». ¡El manirroto! ¡El débil! Y no había calamidad que no remediase . . ., ni niños que no amparase, porque . . ., porque tenía el corazón más grande que hombre tuvo . . . el alma cristiana más pura . . .; no, no, ¡cállate, vieja! ¡Cállate, habladora, y respeta la voluntad de Dios! ¡Arruinadas! Muy bien, y ¡silencio!; pero te veo a ti . . .

ROSITA. No se preocupe de mí, tía. Yo sé que la hipoteca la hizo para pagar mis muebles y mi ajuar, y esto es lo que me duele.

TÍA. Hizo bien. Te lo merecías todo. Y todo lo que se compró es digno de ti y será hermoso el día que lo uses.

ROSITA. ¿El día que lo use?

TÍA. ¡Claro! El día de tu boda.

ROSITA. No me haga usted hablar.

AUNT. God bless you!

She sits down slowly. ROSITA *appears with a bundle of letters. Silence.*

Have they taken the bureau?

ROSITA. Just a moment ago. Your cousin Esperanza sent a child to get a screwdriver.

AUNT. They'll be getting the beds ready for tonight. We should have gone to arrange things as we want them. My cousin will have put the furniture any old how.

ROSITA. I'd rather leave when it's dark. I'd put the street lamp out if I could. The neighbours are sure to be watching. With the removal men here, there's been a crowd of children at the door all day, as if there were a corpse in the house.

AUNT. If I'd only known, I'd never have let your uncle mortgage the house, not to mention the furniture. We are left with the barest necessities – a few chairs and our beds to sleep in!

ROSITA. Or to die in.

AUNT. What a mess he's left us in! The new people coming in tomorrow. I wish he could see us! The old fool! No head for business! Roses on the brain! No concept of money! He was ruining us day by day! He'd say to me: 'Oh, Mr So-and-so's here. Show him in.' And Mr So-and-so would arrive with empty pockets and leave with them stuffed with money. And my husband would say: 'Don't mention it to my wife!' The spendthrift! So easily persuaded! And there was no misfortune he wouldn't try to put right, no child he wouldn't try to help . . . because he was so kind-hearted . . . the purest Christian soul . . . Oh, shut up, you stupid old woman! Stop all this chattering and respect the will of God! Ruined, yes, but we have to accept it . . . Yet when I look at you . . .

ROSITA. Don't worry about me. I know the mortgage was to pay for my furniture and my trousseau. That's what hurts most.

AUNT. It was the right thing to do. You deserved everything. And the things we bought will look a treat the day you use them.

ROSITA. What do you mean?

AUNT. Why, on your wedding day, of course.

ROSITA. I'd rather not talk about it.

TÍA. Ése es el defecto de las mujeres decentes de estas tierras.
¡No hablar! No hablamos y tenemos que hablar. (*A voces.*)
¡Ama! ¿Ha llegado el correo?

ROSITA. ¿Qué se propone usted?

TÍA. Que me veas vivir, para que aprendas.

ROSITA (*abrazándola*). Calle.

TÍA. Alguna vez tengo que hablar alto. Sal de tus cuatro
paredes, hija mía. No te hagas a la desgracia.

ROSITA (*arrodillada delante de ella*). Me he acostumbrado a
vivir muchos años fuera de mí, pensando en cosas que
estaban muy lejos, y ahora que estas cosas ya no existen sigo
dando vueltas y más vueltas por un sitio frío, buscando una
salida que no he de encontrar nunca. Yo lo sabía todo.
Sabía que se había casado; ya se encargó un alma caritativa
de decírmelo; y he estado recibiendo sus cartas con una
ilusión llena de sollozos que aun a mí misma me asombraba.
Si la gente no hubiera hablado; si vosotras no lo hubierais
sabido; si no lo hubiera sabido nadie más que yo, sus
cartas y su mentira hubieran alimentado mi ilusión como el
primer año de su ausencia. Pero lo sabían todos y yo me
encontraba señalada por un dedo que hacía ridícula mi
modestia de prometida y daba un aire grotesco a mi abanico
de soltera. Cada año que pasaba era como una prenda
íntima que arrancaran de mi cuerpo. Y hoy se casa una
amiga y otra y otra, y mañana tiene un hijo y crece, y viene
a enseñarme sus notas de examen, y hacen casas nuevas
y canciones nuevas, y yo igual, con el mismo temblor,
igual; yo, lo mismo que antes, cortando el mismo clavel,
viendo las mismas nubes; y un día bajo al paseo y me doy
cuenta de que no conozco a nadie; muchachas y muchachos
me dejan atrás porque me canso, y uno dice: «Ahí está la
solterona»; y otro, hermoso, con la cabeza rizada, que
comenta: «A ésa ya no hay quien le clave el diente». Y yo lo
oigo y no puedo gritar, sino vamos adelante, con la boca
llena de veneno y con unas ganas enormes de huir, de
quitarme los zapatos, de descansar y no moverme más,
nunca, de mi rincón.

TÍA. ¡Hija! ¡Rosita!

ROSITA. Ya soy vieja. Ayer le oí decir al ama que todavía podía

AUNT. That's the trouble with well-bred women around here: not speaking out. They don't speak when they should. (*Calling out.*) Has the post arrived?

ROSITA. What do you propose?

AUNT. That you see how I'm living, so you learn from my example.

ROSITA (*embracing her*). Shhhh!

AUNT. I have to say what's on my mind. Escape from these four walls, my child! Don't be beaten by misfortune!

ROSITA (*kneeling before her*). For many years I've grown accustomed to living outside myself, thinking about things that were far away. And now that they no longer exist, I find myself going round and round in a cold place, looking for a way out that I know I'll never find. I knew the truth. I knew he'd got married. A well-meaning person insisted on telling me, but I went on receiving his letters with a sense of hope that was full of sorrow. It surprised even me. If no one had said anything; if you hadn't known; if only I had known the truth, his letters and his lies would have gone on feeding my hope just as they did the first year after he left. But everyone knew the truth, and I'd find myself picked out by a pointing finger that made a mockery of my engagement. Each passing year became like an intimate piece of clothing torn from my body. One day a friend gets married, then another, and then another, and the next day she has a child, and the child grows up and comes to show me his examination marks. Or there are new houses and new songs. But I stay the same, with the same trembling excitement; cutting the same carnations; looking up at the same clouds. And one day I'm out walking, and I suddenly realise I don't know anyone. Girls and boys leave me behind because I can't keep up with them, and one of them says: 'Look, there's the old maid.' And another one, a good-looking boy with curly hair, says: 'No one's going to fancy her.' I have to listen to it all, and I can't protest. I have to carry on, but with a mouth full of bitterness and a desperate longing to run away, to take off my shoes, to rest and curl up for ever in my corner.

AUNT. Rosita, my child!

ROSITA. I'm far too old now. Yesterday I heard the

yo casarme. De ningún modo. No lo pienses. Ya perdí la esperanza de hacerlo con quien quise con toda mi sangre, con quien quise y . . . con quien quiero. Todo está acabado . . . y, sin embargo, con toda la ilusión perdida, me acuesto, y me levanto con el más terrible de los sentimientos, que es el sentimiento de tener la esperanza muerta. Quiero huir, quiero no ver, quiero quedarme serena, vacía . . . (¿es que no tiene derecho una pobre mujer a respirar con libertad?) Y, sin embargo, la esperanza me persigue, me ronda, me muerde; como un lobo moribundo que apretara sus dientes por última vez.

TÍA. ¿Por qué no me hiciste caso? ¿Por qué no te casaste con otro?

ROSITA. Estaba atada, y además, ¿qué hombre vino a esta casa sincero y desbordante para procurarse mi cariño? Ninguno.

TÍA. Tú no les hacías ningún caso. Tú estabas encelada por un palomo ladrón.

ROSITA. Yo he sido siempre seria.

TÍA. Te has aferrado a tu idea sin ver la realidad y sin tener caridad de tu porvenir.

ROSITA. Soy como soy. Y no me puedo cambiar. Ahora lo único que me queda es mi dignidad. Lo que tengo por dentro lo guardo para mí sola.

TÍA. Eso es lo que yo no quiero.

AMA (*saliendo de pronto*). ¡Ni yo tampoco! Tú hablas, te desahogas, nos hartamos de llorar las tres y nos repartimos el sentimiento.

ROSITA. ¿Y qué os voy a decir? Hay cosas que no se pueden decir porque no hay palabras para decirlas; y si las hubiera, nadie entendería su significado. Me entendéis si pido pan y agua y hasta un beso, pero nunca me podríais ni entender ni quitar esta mano oscura que no sé si me hiela o me abrasa el corazón cada vez que me quedo sola.

AMA. Ya estás diciendo algo.

TÍA. Para todo hay consuelo.

ROSITA. Sería el cuento de nunca acabar. Yo sé que los ojos los tendré siempre jóvenes, y sé que la espalda se me irá curvando cada día. Después de todo, lo que me ha pasado le ha pasado a mil mujeres. (*Pausa.*) Pero ¿por qué estoy yo hablando todo esto? (*Al* AMA.) Tú, vete a arreglar cosas, que dentro de unos momentos salimos de este carmen; y usted, tía, no se preocupe

housekeeper say I could still get married. I shan't. Don't give it a thought. I lost that hope when I lost the man I wanted with all my soul, the man I loved . . . and go on loving. It's all finished! And yet, though I go to bed knowing that there is no hope, I wake with the most terrible feeling of all, the feeling that hope is finally dead. I want to run away from it, to close my eyes to it, to be calm, empty . . . (Doesn't a poor woman have the right to breathe?) Yet it pursues me, circles around me, gnaws at me; like a dying wolf trying to sink its teeth in for the last time.

AUNT. Why didn't you listen to me? Why didn't you marry someone else?

ROSITA. My hands were tied. And what other man ever came to this house with a genuine wish to win my affection? Not one!

AUNT. You ignored them. You were too dazzled by that honey-tongued liar of yours!

ROSITA. Aunt, I've always been serious about things.

AUNT. You've always clung to that one idea, with no regard for reality and no thought for your own future.

ROSITA. I am what I am. I can't change. All I have left is my dignity. What I feel inside I keep to myself.

AUNT. But that's what I don't want!

HOUSEKEEPER (*suddenly appearing*). Nor me! Speak out! Get things off your chest! We'll all have a good cry, share what we feel!

ROSITA. What can I say to you? There are things we can never say because the words don't exist, and even if they did, no one would understand. You know what I mean if I ask for bread and water or even a kiss, but you'll never understand or be able to remove this dark, heavy hand that freezes or burns my heart – I'm never sure which – whenever I'm alone.

HOUSEKEEPER. Well at least you are making a start.

AUNT. There's always a silver lining.

ROSITA. If I told you the whole story, it would never end. I know my eyes will always be young and my back more bent with every passing day. What's happened to me has happened to thousands of others. (*Pause.*) But why am I saying all this? (*To the* HOUSEKEEPER.) Go and tidy up!

de mí. (*Pausa. Al* AMA.) ¡Vamos! No me agrada que me miréis así. Me molestan esas miradas de perros fieles. (*Se va el* AMA.) Esas miradas de lástima que me perturban y me indignan.

TÍA. Hija, ¿qué quieres que yo haga?

ROSITA. Dejadme como cosa perdida. (*Pausa. Se pasea.*) Ya sé que se está usted acordando de su hermana la solterona . . ., solterona como yo. Era agria y odiaba a los niños y a toda la que se ponía un traje nuevo . . ., pero yo no seré así. (*Pausa.*) Le pido perdón.

TÍA. ¡Qué tontería!

Aparece por el fondo de la habitación un MUCHACHO *de dieciocho años.*

ROSITA. Adelante.

MUCHACHO. Pero ¿se mudan ustedes?

ROSITA. Dentro de unos minutos. Al oscurecer.

TÍA. ¿Quién es?

ROSITA. Es el hijo de María.

TÍA. ¿Qué María?

ROSITA. La mayor de las tres Manolas.

TÍA. ¡Ah!

Las que suben a la Alhambra
las tres y las cuatro solas.

Perdona, hijo, mi mala memoria.

MUCHACHO. Me ha visto usted muy pocas veces.

TÍA. Claro, pero quería mucho a tu madre. ¡Qué graciosa era! Murió por la misma época que mi marido.

ROSITA. Antes.

MUCHACHO. Hace ocho años.

ROSITA. Y tiene la misma cara.

MUCHACHO (*alegre*). Un poquito peor. Yo la tengo hecha a martillazos.

TÍA. Y las mismas salidas; ¡el mismo genio!

MUCHACHO. Pero claro que me parezco. En carnaval me puse un vestido de mi madre . . . un vestido del año de la nana, verde . . .

ROSITA (*melancólica*). Con lazos negros . . . y bullones de seda verde nilo.

MUCHACHO. Sí.

ROSITA. Y un gran lazo de terciopelo en la cintura.

We'll be leaving this house shortly. And you, Aunt, you are not to worry. (*Pause. To the* HOUSEKEEPER.) Go on! I can't bear the way you look at me, like some faithful dog. (*The* HOUSEKEEPER *goes out.*) These pitying looks, they upset me. They make me angry.

AUNT. Child, what am I to do?

ROSITA. Accept me as a hopeless cause. (*Pause. Walks up and down.*) I know I remind you of your sister, another old maid. She was a very bitter person – hated children and any girl with a new dress. But I shan't be like her. (*Pause.*) I'm sorry.

AUNT. Oh, don't be silly!

An eighteen-year-old boy enters.

ROSITA. Come in.

YOUTH. Are you moving, then?

ROSITA. In a few minutes. When it gets dark.

AUNT. Who is he?

ROSITA. Maria's son.

AUNT. Which Maria?

ROSITA. The eldest of the three Manolas.

AUNT. Ah!

They visit the Alhambra
Alone, in twos, or threes.

You'll have to excuse me, child. My memory's very bad.

YOUTH. You've only seen me a couple of times.

AUNT. I was very fond of your mother. A really charming person. She died at about the same time as my husband.

ROSITA. It was before that.

YOUTH. It was eight years ago.

ROSITA. He has her features.

YOUTH (*with spirit*). But not as nice as hers. Mine were put together with a hammer.

AUNT. Well, the same sense of humour, anyway.

YOUTH. I suppose I *do* look like her. During carnival once I put on one of her dresses . . . one she'd had for ages . . . a green one.

ROSITA (*sadly*). With black lace . . . and flounces of Nile-green silk.

YOUTH. Yes.

ROSITA. And a big velvet bow at the waist.

MUCHACHO. El mismo.

ROSITA. Que cae a un lado y otro del polisón.

MUCHACHO. ¡Exacto! ¡Qué disparate de moda! (*Se sonríe.*)

ROSITA (*triste*). ¡Era una moda bonita!

MUCHACHO. ¡No me diga usted! Pues bajaba yo muerto de risa
    con el vejestorio puesto, llenando todo el pasillo de la casa de
    olor de alcanfor, y de pronto mi tía se puso a llorar
    amargamente porque decía que era exactamente igual que
    ver a mi madre. Yo me impresioné, como es natural, y dejé el
    traje y el antifaz sobre mi cama.

ROSITA. Como que no hay cosa más viva que un recuerdo.
    Llegan a hacernos la vida imposible. Por eso yo comprendo
    muy bien a esas viejecillas borrachas que van por las calles
    queriendo borrar el mundo, y se sientan a cantar en los
    bancos del paseo.

TÍA. ¿Y tu tía la casada?

MUCHACHO. Escribe desde Barcelona. Cada vez menos.

ROSITA. ¿Tiene hijos?

MUCHACHO. Cuatro.

    Pausa.

AMA (*entrando*). Déme usted las llaves del armario. (*La* TÍA *se
    las da. Por el* MUCHACHO.) Aquí, el joven, iba ayer con su
    novia. Los vi por la Plaza Nueva. Ella quería ir por un lado y
    él no la dejaba. (*Ríe.*)

TÍA. ¡Vamos con el niño!

MUCHACHO (*azorado*). Estábamos de broma.

AMA. ¡No te pongas colorado! (*Saliendo.*)

ROSITA. ¡Vamos, calla!

MUCHACHO. ¡Qué jardín más precioso tienen ustedes!

ROSITA. ¡Teníamos!

TÍA. Ven, y corta unas flores.

MUCHACHO. Usted lo pase bien, doña Rosita.

ROSITA. ¡Anda con Dios, hijo! (*Salen. La tarde está cayendo.*)
    ¡Doña Rosita! ¡Doña Rosita!

    Cuando se abre en la mañana
    roja como sangre está.

YOUTH. That's the one.

ROSITA. Falling on either side of the bustle.

YOUTH. Such a silly fashion! (*He laughs.*)

ROSITA (*sadly*). But so pretty!

YOUTH. Anyway, there I was, coming down the stairs, in the dress, laughing my head off, filling the place with the smell of mothballs, and all of a sudden my aunt started to cry, because she said it was just like seeing my mother. Well, that set me off too, so I left the dress and the mask on my bed.

ROSITA. Nothing is more alive than a memory. In the end they make our lives impossible. That's why I can understand those little old women who take to drink and wander the streets trying to blot out the world, or sit on the seats along the avenue, singing to themselves.

AUNT. How is your married aunt?

YOUTH. She writes to us from Barcelona. Not as often as she used to, though.

ROSITA. Does she have any children?

YOUTH. She's got four.

> *Pause.*

HOUSEKEEPER (*entering*). I need the keys to the wardrobe. (*The* AUNT *gives her the keys. Then, referring to the boy:*) This one was with his sweetheart yesterday. I saw them in the Plaza Nueva. She wanted to walk one way and he was trying to stop her. (*Laughs.*)

AUNT. Let the poor boy be!

YOUTH (*embarrassed*). It was only a bit of fun.

HOUSEKEEPER (*leaving*). Why are you blushing, then?

ROSITA. That's quite enough!

YOUTH. You've got a very nice garden.

ROSITA. You mean we used to.

AUNT. Come, we'll cut some flowers.

YOUTH. I'd like to wish you the best of luck, Doña Rosita.

ROSITA. God be with you, child.

> *The* AUNT *and the* YOUTH *go out. It is getting dark.*

Doña Rosita! Doña Rosita!

She opens in the morning,
Her colour red and deep.

La tarde la pone blanca
con blanco de espuma y sal.
Y cuando llega la noche
se comienza a deshojar.

Pausa.

AMA (*sale con un chal*). ¡En marcha!

ROSITA. Sí, voy a echarme un abrigo.

AMA. Como he descolgado la percha, lo tienes enganchado en el tirador de la ventana.

Entra la SOLTERONA 3a, *vestida de oscuro, con un velo de luto en la cabeza y la pena, que se llevaba en el año doce. Hablan bajo.*

SOLTERONA 3a. ¡Ama!

AMA. Por unos minutos nos encuentra aquí.

SOLTERONA 3a. Yo vengo a dar una lección de piano que tengo aquí cerca y me llegué por si necesitaban ustedes algo.

AMA. ¡Dios se lo pague!

SOLTERONA 3a. ¡Qué cosa más grande!

AMA. Sí, sí, pero no me toque usted el corazón, no me levante la gasa de la pena, porque yo soy la que tiene que dar ánimos en este duelo sin muerto que está usted presenciando.

SOLTERONA 3a. Yo quisiera saludarlas.

AMA. Pero es mejor que no las vea. ¡Vaya por la otra casa!

SOLTERONA 3a. Es mejor. Pero si hace falta algo, ya sabe que, en lo que pueda, aquí estoy yo.

AMA. ¡Ya pasará la mala hora!

Se oye el viento.

SOLTERONA 3a. ¡Se ha levantado un aire!

AMA. Sí. Parece que va a llover.

La SOLTERONA 3a *se va.*

TÍA (*entra*). Como siga este viento no va a quedar una rosa viva. Los cipreses de la glorieta casi tocan las paredes de mi cuarto. Parece como si alguien quisiera poner el jardín feo para que no tuviésemos pena de dejarlo.

AMA. Como precioso, precioso, no ha sido nunca. ¿Se ha puesto su abrigo? Y esta nube. Así, bien tapada. (*Se la pone.*)

When evening comes her colour fades,
Pale as a salt-stained cheek.
When darkness falls, her life ends,
Her lovely petals start to weep.

Pause.

HOUSEKEEPER (*entering, wrapped in a shawl*). Time to go!
ROSITA. I'll get my coat.
HOUSEKEEPER. I've taken the coat-rack down. Your coat's on
the window-catch.

The THIRD SPINSTER *enters. She is wearing a dark dress
with a mourning veil over her head and a ribbon around
her neck in the style of 1912. They speak quietly.*

THIRD SPINSTER. Excuse me!
HOUSEKEEPER. We are leaving in a few minutes.
THIRD SPINSTER. I'm giving a piano lesson nearby. I called to
see if you needed anything.
HOUSEKEEPER. May God reward you.
THIRD SPINSTER. What a sad day this is!
HOUSEKEEPER. Yes, yes. But don't make me go all weepy now.
Don't expose the painful wound! I'm the one who has to put
some life into this funeral, even though there's no dead body.
THIRD SPINSTER. I'd like to say hello to them.
HOUSEKEEPER. Better not. Call at the other house.
THIRD SPINSTER. Yes, that would be better. But if you need
anything, you know I'll do what I can.
HOUSEKEEPER. It's a bad time, but things will get better.

The wind is heard.

THIRD SPINSTER. The wind's rising.
HOUSEKEEPER. It looks like rain.

The THIRD SPINSTER *leaves.*

AUNT (*entering*). With all this wind there won't be a rose left.
The cypresses by the summer-house are almost touching the
walls of my room. Perhaps someone wanted to make the
garden ugly, so we wouldn't feel sad at leaving it behind.
HOUSEKEEPER. It was never that pretty! Is your coat on
properly? And your scarf? (*Helps her with it.*) There! All

Ahora, cuando lleguemos, tengo la comida hecha. De postre, flan. A usted le gusta. Un flan dorado como una clavellina. (*El* AMA *habla con la voz velada por una profunda emoción.*)

Se oye un golpe.

TÍA. Es la puerta del invernadero. ¿Por qué no la cierras?

AMA. No se puede cerrar por la humedad.

TÍA. Estará toda la noche golpeando.

AMA. ¡Como no la oiremos . . .!

La escena está en una dulce penumbra de atardecer.

TÍA. Yo, sí. Yo sí la oiré.

Aparece ROSITA. *Viene pálida, vestida de blanco, con un abrigo hasta el filo del vestido.*

AMA (*valiente*). ¡Vamos!

ROSITA (*con voz débil*). Ha empezado a llover. Así no habrá nadie en los balcones para vernos salir.

TÍA. Es preferible.

ROSITA (*vacila un poco, se apoya en una silla y cae sostenida por el* AMA *y la* TÍA, *que impiden su total desmayo*).
Y cuando llega la noche
se comienza a deshojar.

Salen y a su mutis queda la escena sola. Se oye golpear la puerta. De pronto se abre un balcón del fondo y las blancas cortinas oscilan con el viento.

Telón.

done! I've got a meal ready for when we get there. Custard for dessert, the way you like it. As golden as a marigold!

The HOUSEKEEPER *speaks in a voice choked with emotion. Something is heard banging.*

AUNT. The greenhouse door! Can't you close it?
HOUSEKEEPER. It won't close. It's swollen with the rain.
AUNT. It'll bang all night.
HOUSEKEEPER. Well, we shan't hear it . . .!

The stage is in the soft half-light of evening.

AUNT. But I will! I will!

ROSITA *enters. She looks pale and is dressed in white, her coat down to the hem of her dress.*

HOUSEKEEPER (*bravely*). Let's go.
ROSITA (*weakly*). It's started to rain. No one will be watching.
AUNT. Much better if they aren't.
ROSITA (*hesitates, holds on to the back of a chair, almost faints but is supported by the* HOUSEKEEPER *and the* AUNT.)
And when darkness surrounds her,
Her petals start to fall.

They leave and the stage is left empty. The door is heard banging. Suddenly, the french window at the back of the stage blows open and the white curtains flutter in the wind.

Curtain.

Notes

Act One

1   The title of the play is extremely elaborate: *Doña Rosita the Spinster or The Language of the Flowers. A poem of Granada in 1900, divided into various gardens, with scenes of song and dance.* In the play itself Rosita is not called 'Doña Rosita' until the Youth addresses her as such towards the end of Act Three. The title 'Doña' is one applied to an older woman as a mark of respect, but although that is what the Youth intends, we can well imagine that others would use the term in order to mock her as she visibly ages. We should note that, as in the case of *Yerma*, Lorca calls the play a poem. There is, indeed, a good deal of poetry in the play, either read aloud or recited from memory, but *Doña Rosita* is also a poem in the sense that Rosita's inner life is revealed to us in a highly emotional and moving manner, as in a lyric poem.

5   *Hellebore*: there are various kinds of hellebore. They have yellow-green, white, or purple flowers and appear in late winter or early spring.

5   *violet Louis-Passy* : I have failed to find any reference anywhere to either the violet Louis-Passy, which is clearly named after this particular individual, or to the 'altair', which in all reference books is described as a star of a bluish colour. It could, of course, describe a star-like flower. But it seems quite possible that the Aunt is here simply mocking the Uncle by producing a list of flowers with which she is only vaguely familiar and which, in some cases, she simply gets wrong. The flower which she calls 'altair' could possibly be the *althea* or hollyhock, which has white to pink or purple flowers.

5   *heliotrope*: the heliotrope has small white or purplish fragrant flowers.

5   *Countess of Wandes*: the single-flowered moss rose or

musk rose came from England, where it was cultivated for the first time in 1807 in the gardens of the Countess of Wandes in Bayswater, London.

5   *quince*: a hard, sharp, yellowish fruit, not unlike an apple.

5   *in my village*: it is not really clear whether or not the Housekeeper has accommodation in the Aunt and Uncle's house or whether she lives elsewhere. The village is probably where she was born, and, given the fact that she is of a similar age to the Aunt, the later reference to her children living in poverty also seems to allude to the past. If she does not have a room in the Aunt and Uncle's house, she could well live nearby. As in the case of Poncia in *The House of Bernarda Alba*, Lorca partly based the Housekeeper on Dolores Cuesta, who had worked for his family for many years.

7   *in the style of 1900*: Lorca had stated in an interview in late 1934 that the three acts of the play are set in 1890, 1900 and 1910 respectively. The reference to 1900 for Act One is therefore a clear slip on his part.

7   *leg-of-mutton sleeves*: sleeves which are very full on the upper arm but narrow down the forearm.

7   *San Luis*: this was a church in the Albaicín which was largely destroyed during the Civil War. The Aunt and Uncle probably live quite close by.

7   *doing some lace-work, embroidering a cap?*: translated literally, the sentence here would read very awkwardly: 'When have you ever seen her sit down to make tatting or frivolité or garland points or drawn work to adorn a cap?' 'Tatting' is a lace-like threadwork, 'garland points' decorative bands hanging in a curve between two points, 'Frivolité' a form of tatting.

7   *shout to sheet and sheet to shout*: the Spanish phrase 'del coro al caño y del caño al coro' means 'from the wine-cellar to the choir (or chancel)', in other words, 'from one extreme to another'. It is important to suggest in the translation, given the Aunt's comment in the following line, that the Housekeeper's 'sheet' could easily become 'shit'.

9   *hispid*: there is no reference to the hispid rose in any of

the reference books, including the Royal Horticultural
Society's *Gardener's Encyclopedia of Plants and
Flowers*.

9   *Queen Elizabeth eglantine*: a type of thorny rose with
pink flowers and apple-scented foliage.

9   *inermis*: this refers to the stem of the *rosa declinata*
which, unlike the stem of most roses, has no thorns.

9   *myrtifolia*: related to the myrtle family.

9   *sulfurata*: has a bright yellow flower, the colour of
sulphur.

9   *rosa mutabilis*: this is a rose which has yellow flowers
that change with time to coppery-pink or crimson, but
the rose described by the Uncle is evidently one which
only he has succeeded in cultivating.

11   *By Saint Bartholomew's wheel*: for all her practicality,
the Housekeeper, like many uneducated working-class
women of the time, is as superstitious as she is religious.
Saint Bartholomew was one of the twelve apostles,
though he was not normally associated with a wheel. He
was either flayed to death or crucified. He is the patron
saint of butchers and in art is often represented holding a
knife. Saint Joseph was, of course, the husband of Mary
and foster-father of Jesus. During the seventeenth
century the cult of Joseph was strongly supported by the
Jesuits and, especially in Spain, by Saint Teresa of Avila.

11   *From Jerusalem's holy land*: literally, 'from Jerusalem's
four corners'.

11   *Shi . . . Shame on you!*: in the Spanish text the
Housekeeper begins the equivalent word with 'ca', and
was probably going to say 'caca' ('shit'), which she
quickly changes to the innocuous 'caramba' ('Good
heavens!).

13   *Manolas*: the word describes a high-spirited young
woman, aware of her beauty and wearing a lace
mantilla, with a high comb in her hair. In the time of
Goya she was known as a *maja* (see his paintings, *Majas
on a Balcony* and *Majas Walking*).

13   *bobbins*: small cylinders around which thread or yarn is
wound and can be unwound with ease. For use in
weaving or sewing.

13   *a niche in the wall*: literally, 'a niche of crystals and
      snow', evidently a display case.
13   *I've devoted my life . . .*: the original is in the form of a
      command: 'Bring up a girl for this . . .'
13   *a wretched hovel*: this anticipates the Servant's
      complaint in Act One of *The House of Bernarda Alba*:
      'A bitter pill to swallow for those of us who live in huts
      of mud, with a plate and a spoon.' It points very clearly
      to the social and economic divide between the rich and
      the poor in late nineteenth-century and early twentieth-
      century Spain, and also to Lorca's life-long compassion
      for the poor.
13   *camomile*: an aromatic herb whose flowers and leaves
      are used in medicine. Camomile tea, for example, has a
      calming effect. Near Granada's cathedral, in the street
      called Cárcel Baja, there is still an open-air market where
      herbal remedies can be purchased.
15   *Tucumán*: a province of north-western Argentina,
      covering an area of 8.697 square miles. The eastern part
      of the province is flat and productive. In the early
      nineteenth century, sugarcane became the most
      important agricultural product, but beans, lemons,
      potatoes and tobacco were also cultivated. This is
      doubtless where the Nephew's father has his land and
      where, in the Aunt's words, he will become 'a farmer'.
15   *A poisoned arrow*: the Spanish text has 'an arrow with
      purple ribbons'. Purple is a colour associated with
      sadness, suffering, and death.
15   *admiring the flowers*: in the Spanish text the phrase
      translates literally, 'Here you are nothing more than a
      passer-by in the little gardens'. This is a good example of
      the need to avoid a strictly literal translation.
15   *over my dead body*: literally, 'You'd have to jump over
      me and your uncle'.
15   *I should have been struck dumb*: literally, 'My tongue
      should have stuck to the roof of my mouth'.
17   *don't confuse respect with shamelessness*: he means that
      the Aunt should realise that respect for his father's
      wishes does not mean that he is shamelessly abandoning
      Rosita.

17   *beg in the streets*: literally, 'Begging in the streets for
     ochavitos'. An *ochavo* was an old coin of little value,
     similar to the old British farthing.

17   *sesame seed*: the sesame plant, cultivated for its seeds,
     was once thought to have magical powers.

17   *cinnamon flower*: cinnamon comes from the aromatic
     inner bark of a tropical tree of the laurel family and is
     used as a spice.

17   *St Nicholas' well*: St Nicholas was a fourth-century
     prelate, bishop of Myra. He was the patron saint of
     Russia, seamen, and children, and, in Dutch nursery
     lore, is, of course, Santa Claus. There seems to be no
     logical meaning to the Housekeeper's spell. It is almost
     like a children's rhyme, a piece of nonsense.

19   The poetic lines which follow have throughout the
     typical pattern of Spanish assonance, each alternate line,
     from 'de mis tres lindas Manolas's, ending 'Manolas',
     'ronda', 'boca', 'colcha', the principal stress falling on
     the 'o'. It is impossible to retain this pattern in English
     but important to preserve the lyrical flow of the passage.

19   *You should tie each sigh with a ribbon*: this suggests
     tying together love letters, and anticipates the letters
     which Rosita later receives from the Nephew.

21   *I've heard things/about you*: there would doubtless have
     been considerable gossip about the visits of the Manolas
     to the Alhambra, particularly at night. Lorca frequently
     refers to the gossip which unconventional behaviour
     invited in Granada and in Spain in general. Bernarda
     Alba's daughters allude to it, and Yerma's husband,
     Juan, is greatly concerned that her wilful behaviour leads
     to it. Lorca was, of course, himself the victim of such
     gossip as a result of his early association with the artistic
     group at the Café Alameda and, later on, his
     homosexuality.

21   *Elvira Street*: it lies in the heart of Granada, some 500
     yards below the Alhambra and runs parallel to the city's
     main avenue, the Gran Vía de Colón. Before the
     construction of the Gran Vía at the end of the nineteenth
     century, Elvira Street was the main thoroughfare in the
     city.

21 *the Alhambra*: although the Moorish palaces had fallen
    into gradual decline during the eighteenth and most of
    the nineteenth centuries, repair and restoration began in
    1870 when they were finally recognised as a national
    monument. Lorca, as Rosita's lines suggest, presents the
    Alhambra in a Romantic light, reminiscent of the way in
    which it had been described by the nineteenth-century
    writers mentioned in the Commentary (pp. xxi–xxv).

21 *bodice*: the Spanish text has 'Scottish bodice'. It is not
    clear whether this refers to the type or to the pattern of
    this particular bodice.

21 *the leaping fountain*: the reference to water could be to
    any part of the Alhambra where fountains are to be
    found both inside and outside the palaces.

21 *myrtle*: a plant which was sacred to Venus and therefore
    associated with love.

21 *The cathedral lies in darkness/and the breeze softly
    sings*: literally, 'the cathedral has left/ bronzes which the
    breeze accepts'. The meaning is obscure. Granada's
    cathedral is in the city, well below the Alhambra. Rosita
    may be referring to the Church of Santa María de la
    Alhambra, completed in 1617, which stands in the
    grounds of the Alhambra, to the right of the Palace of
    Charles V.

23 *The Genil . . . / The Dauro*: these are Granada's two
    rivers. In Granada itself, the Dauro runs beneath the
    Calle Reyes Católicos and joins up with the Genil a short
    distance away. In Lorca's time, the Dauro was not
    completely underground, as it is today. Rosita is clearly
    referring to the rivers outside the city, where there are
    oxen and butterflies.

23 *Our bridal petticoats/Are edged with frost*: an
    anticipation of Rosita's abandonment by her cousin and
    of the bridal gown which will be left unused.

25 *Alhambra of jasmine*: jasmine has fragrant and usually
    white flowers. It symbolises the beauty of the Alhambra,
    especially in the moonlight, but also evokes its
    melancholy and sadness.

25 *Where the moon sleeps*: the moon is one of Lorca's
    favourite images, prominent in both his poetry and his

plays, and frequently associated with fate and death. In
Act Three of *Blood Wedding*, for example, Moon
conspires with Death to bring about the deaths of the
Bridegroom and Leonardo.

25   *Come with me. I'll tell you what's happened*: see the
Commentary (p. lxxiii) on how the following dialogue
between Rosita and the Nephew might be the Manolas'
interpretation of that episode, transformed in their
imagination into a highly stylised, poetic encounter.

25   *Czerny étude*: Karl Czerny (1766–1817) was an Austrian
composer and pianist. The piano accompaniment to the
scene creates an extremely romantic mood, as in an old
film. We should not forget that Lorca was himself a very
accomplished pianist.

27   *Oh, why did our eyes ever meet . . . ?*: as stated in the
Commentary (p. lxxiii), I have toned down somewhat
the sentimentality of the original, which would probably
not work in a modern English production. In an earlier
translation – see *Lorca Plays: One* – Rosita's opening
lines were as follows:

> When your eyes met mine, cousin.
> They did so treacherously.
> When your hands gave me flowers, cousin,
> They did so deceitfully.
> And now, still young, you are leaving me
> To the nightingale's sad song.
> You, whom I loved so truly,
> Can only do me this wrong.
> How can you leave me so cruelly,
> Like the strings of a lute struck dumb?

27   *nightingale's/sad song*: the male nightingale was noted
for its melodious song at night. Lorca frequently alludes
to it as an indication of sadness and loneliness.

27   *vis-à-vis*: a double seat in the shape of an 's', designed to
allow two people to sit while facing each other.

27   *My garden*: this is the enclosed garden of the 'carmen',
the house in the Albaicín where Rosita lives with the
Aunt and Uncle. On the 'carmen', see the Commentary,
p. xxv–xxvi.

27 *red as wallflower*: the wallflower can be bronze, orange, red, and various other colours. In both his poetry and plays Lorca often referred to flowers as metaphors for bleeding wounds.

29 *Whenever my horse grazes*: the following lines evoke the large estate on which the Nephew will work for his father. Lorca visited Argentina in 1933.

29 *longing for / The sea*: Granada is a land-locked city, separated and cut off from the sea by the massive mountain range of the Sierra Nevada to the south. For Lorca the sea represented freedom and openness, in contrast to the physical and mental claustrophobia of his home town.

29 *lemon groves*: for Lorca the lemon signified bitterness and here points to the anguish in store for Rosita.

31 *embroider sheets*: these are the sheets for the marriage-bed. In Act Two of *The House of Bernarda Alba*, the daughters embroider sheets for Angustias, soon to be married to Pepe el Romano.

Act Two

35 *Mr X*: Lorca's brother has suggested that Mr X is based on various university professors known to Lorca, including the highly distinguished teacher and writer, José Ortega y Gasset.

35 *The century we've just begun*: for Spain, which in 1898 had lost Cuba and the Philippines, the last remnants of a once-great empire, the beginning of the twentieth century was a time of disaster. Mr X, though satirised by Lorca, has a more expansive view of things, for he looks beyond his own country to the progress which is being made worldwide.

35 *Panhard-Levassor*: René Panhard, a French automobile engineer and manufacturer, worked with Emile Levassor to produce the first vehicle with an internal combustion engine mounted at the front of the chassis. This was the prototype of the modern motor car, which went on sale in 1892 and took part in early motor races.

35   *Marcel Renault*: with his brothers Louis and Fernand,
     Marcel Renault built a series of small cars and in 1898
     formed the Société Renault Frères, the origin of the
     present-day Renault automobile company, now
     government owned. In 1903 Marcel Renault was killed
     in the Paris–Madrid motor race. If Act Two is set in
     1900, Lorca confused his dates.

35   *positivism*: a way of thinking that considers the facts of
     physical science as the only way of ascertaining the truth
     of anything.

35   *quietist attitudes or obscurantist ideas*: quietism is a
     movement which encourages spiritual exaltation through
     self-denial and contemplation. An obscurantist is one
     who opposes education, enlightenment, and freedom of
     thought.

35   *Jean-Baptiste Say*: a French economist (1767–1832) best
     known for his law of markets, which states that supply
     creates its own demand. His ideas were a central tenet of
     orthodox economies until the Great Depression of the
     1930s.

35   *Count Leo Tolstwa*: Leo Nikolaevich Tolstoy
     (1829–1910), the Russian novelist and social reformer,
     author of *War and Peace*.

35   *polity*: the form or method of government of a nation.
     Mr X supports the liberal ideas of the time.

35   *natura naturata*: the natural phenomena and forces
     whereby creation is manifested.

35   *Santos Dumont*: Alberto Santos Dumont (1873–1932)
     was a Brazilian aviation pioneer. He spent most of his
     life in France and around the turn of the century began
     to build dirigible airships. He later turned his attention
     to power-driven planes.

37   *Brahma*: in Hindu religion, Brahma is the supreme god
     or the absolute primordial essence.

37   *Anthemis*: otherwise known as 'dog fennel', which has
     daisy-like flower heads and fern-like foliage. Some are
     bright orange, others yellow.

37   *pulsatilla*: a perennial plant with large, feathery leaves
     and bell-shaped flowers, which may be white, pale
     yellow or lavender blue.

37   *datura stramonium*: the shrub called *datura* or *brugmansia*, and otherwise known as 'angels' trumpets' comes in various forms, with white, yellow, red, or orange flowers.

37   *saint's day*: in Catholic countries, people are often named after saints and celebrate the feast day of that saint as they would a birthday.

37   *a mother-of-pearl Eiffel Tower*: Mr X's gift is suitably exaggerated by Lorca, an ironic mixture of romantic sentiment – mother-of-pearl – and contemporary progress – the wheel of industry. The Eiffel Tower was, at this time, relatively recent, having been constructed for the Paris Exhibition of 1889.

39   *Don Confucius Montes de Oca*: the surname, Montes de Oca, was that of one of nineteenth-century Spain's best-known military conspirators. The disparity between this impressive surname and the ridiculous Christian name is another example of Lorca's desire to mock Granada's pretentious bourgeoisie. The reference to 'Lodge number 43' indicates that Don Confucius is a Freemason.

39   *a broom upside down*: another of the Housekeeper's superstitious practices, equivalent to her earlier casting of spells.

39   *fifteen years*: if Act One is set in 1890 and Act Two in 1900, the Nephew cannot have been away for fifteen years, which would place Act One in 1885. Lorca was, however, rather careless with his dates, and one wonders if such inaccuracies were corrected in the first productions.

39   *lace*: literally, 'of Marseilles lace'. France was one of the principal lace-making countries in the second half of the nineteenth century.

39   *wearing them out*: in Act Two of *Yerma*, Yerma bitterly observes to her husband that a home is only a home 'when the chairs and the bedsheets get worn out with use'.

41   *Clowns may speak, but they shouldn't bark*: the Spanish word 'zafio', feminine 'zafia', means a crude, rough person. The Aunt is presumably saying that the

Housekeeper is, given her position as a servant, going too far and being too outspoken.

41 *in the style of Louis the fifteenth*: the style of architecture, decoration and furniture in the age of Louis XV (1715–74) marked the culmination of rococo – flowing lines, rounded forms, graceful shells, flowers and other ornamentation. The elaborate object described by the Housekeeper is a perfect example.

45 *make my bed*: the Uncle prefers his own company, to be independent. His devotion to his flowers suggests that he has escaped into a world of his own.

45 *dressed in pink*: the rose-coloured dress of Act One is now paler, paralleling the *rosa mutabilis* fading as time passes.

47 *'Waltz of the Roses'*: there were many waltzes associated with the rose, such as the 'Roses and Thorns Waltz' and the 'Love and Roses Waltz', composed in 1893 and 1913 respectively.

49 *those show-off spinsters*: the Spanish word 'cursi', here applied to the spinsters, means 'affected', 'precious', 'pretentious'. They are, in effect, a grotesque form of Rosita, anticipating in this respect the mockery that will later be directed at her.

49 *Faith! Charity! Mercy!*: in the Spanish text the first of the spinsters is called 'Amor' (Love) but in English this needs to be changed.

49 *purple ribbons*: see note to p. 15 on the significance of purple. The Mother is a widow, appropriately dressed in dark colours.

49 *lavender*: an aromatic shrub of the mint family, from which perfume and oil for the skin can be produced.

49 *boiled mallows*: the mallow is a spreading herb with roundish leaves and small, pale pink flowers. Its leaves are used to make a medicinal tea.

49 *St Francis rose-bush*: when Saint Francis of Assisi received the stigmata, his blood was said to have been transformed into roses when it spilled on the earth. Hence the name of this particular rose-bush.

51 *syringa*: otherwise known as the lilac. It comes in various

forms and colours, ranging from mauve-pink to lilac-
blue, purple-red, white, and violet-purple.

51 *decent money*: literally, 'seventy duros'. A *duro* was a
coin worth five pesetas.

51 *the evening promenade*: the reference is to the Alameda,
a tree-lined avenue in Granada where it was possible to
take a stroll or hire a seat, and where young men and
women could catch each other's eye.

53 *Ponce de León girls*: these were important and well-
known families in the Granada of the period in question,
which is why the Mother makes the unlikely claim that
her daughters know them.

53 *Heaven's Gate School*: the 'Colegio de la Puerta del
Cielo' is known in English-speaking countries as the
'Porta Coeli Convent'.

53 *nainsook*: a soft, lightweight cotton fabric, usually shiny
on one side.

53 *moiré*: a corded silk fabric, with a wavy pattern created
by passing the fabric between engraved cylinders which
press the design into the material.

53 *the high and mighty Ayola*: Francisco García Lorca has
stated that the name 'Ayola, Photographer' appeared at
the bottom of many family photographs in the Lorca
household. The father of the two girls was indeed the
royal photographer.

55 *a peseta a month*: see note to p. 13 on the social and
economic divide between the rich and the poor. In *The
House of Bernarda Alba*, Bernarda, who has much more
money than anyone else in the village, comments
cuttingly: 'The poor are like animals. It's as if they are
made of different stuff.' Peasants working on the land in
1930 earned between two and four pesetas a day – a tiny
amount – for a twelve-hour shift in summer. In Act
Three of *The House of Bernarda Alba*, Bernarda says
that she has spent 16,000 reales (or 4,000 pesetas) on
furniture for Angustias's home after her marriage. So the
difference between those who had money and those who
did not was substantial.

57 *Popper's 'Tarantella'*: David Popper (1843–1913) was
for the most part a composer of cello music. The

tarantella is a lively Neapolitan dance in 6/8 time. It was once thought to be a remedy for 'tarantism', a condition which manifested heightened excitability and restlessness and which was believed to be caused by the bite of the tarantula. Tarantism produced in the affected person an extreme impulse to dance. The disease was prevalent in Apulia and neighbouring parts of Italy from the fifteenth to the seventeenth century.

57 *'The Virgin's Prayer'*: a piece by the Polish composer, Thekle Bederzewska.

57 *Saint Catherine's Bones*: Saint Catherine, a virgin of Alexandria, lived in the fourth century and was put to death on a wheel for professing Christian beliefs. The 'bones' are long, bone-shaped, marzipan sweets with a filling, often of chocolate.

57 *anisette*: an alcoholic cordial made from or flavoured with aniseed, the fragrant seed of the anise plant.

59 *Fifteen!*: see note to p. 39. If the Nephew has been gone for fifteen years and the First Ayola used to call at the house when she was six, this would now make her twenty-one years of age. However, she says she's going to get married as soon as she can, which sounds more like a sixteen-year-old than someone of twenty-one. It seems more likely that she is sixteen years old and that the Nephew has been away for ten years.

61 *'Viva Frascuelo!'*: Salvador Sánchez Povedano, known as 'Frascuelo', was a bullfighter in the province of Granada, born in 1842, died 1898. He participated in 1,236 fights and killed 3,801 bulls.

61 *'The Frigate Numancia'*: problems between Spain and Peru arose in the mid-1860s and led to an alliance between Peru and Chile. *Numancia* was an armoured frigate commissioned by the Spanish. It played a vital part in the conflict and overcame all ships that opposed it. A barcarole is a boat song with a gentle rhythm, reminiscent of the songs of Venetian gondoliers. The most famous barcaroles are from the Romantic period and were included in both grand and light operas by, for example, Verdi, Rossini, Donizetti, Offenbach, and Sullivan.

61 '*What the Flowers Say*': Francisco García Lorca has recalled that Federico had a list, written in a female hand, which explained the symbolic significance of thirty-one flowers, and which might have been given to him by Emilia Llanos. 'What the Flowers Say' contains many of the flowers mentioned in the list, but he also included five others: the dahlia, the lily, the passion-flower, the hyacinth, and the immortelle. At the same time, Lorca could have consulted other popular sources – illustrated books on flowers were extremely popular – and it seems quite likely that the list he was given was, in any case, derived from those.

61 *recites and plays*: this makes it clear that the following verses were spoken rather than sung.

61 '*The dark swallows will soon return . . .*': this is the first line of a famous poem by the nineteenth-century poet, Gustavo Adolfo Bécquer (1836–70).

61 *heliotrope*: see note to p. 5.

61 *basil-flower*: basil is an aromatic plant of the mint family.

61 *jasmine*: a fragrant flower which may be white or pinkish-red in colour.

61 *hyacinth*: there are different kinds of hyacinth, whose colours vary from rose-red to navy-blue and soft pink. The flower is said to have sprung from the blood of Hyacinthus, beloved of Apollo, and to have had on its petals the expressions of grief 'Ai, ai'.

61 *passion-flower*: so called not through any association with love, but because certain parts of the flower resemble the instruments of the Crucifixion. Although here Lorca uses it to signify pain, he later uses it a second time attributing trust to the flower.

63 *mustard-flower*: there are two kinds of mustard-flower: the white and the black mustard. Both are annuals, with yellow flowers and pods of roundish seeds.

63 *spike-nard*: a fragrant perennial of the valerian family, with small white or pink flowers. Like the passion-flower Lorca mentions it twice, the second time spreaking of love's pain.

63 *honeysuckle*: a climbing plant of which there are various

kinds. Its tubular flowers may be white, yellow, pink, red, or purple in colour.

63   *immortelle*: a flower which retains its colour for a long time after it has been picked, hence its name. There are several varieties, with daisy-like flower heads in many colours.

63   *Matching a young girl's sighs*: this is an extra line of my own, intended to rhyme, if not perfectly, with 'Some are as sharp as knives'.

63   *A meaning of their own / Who can understand it?*: for the reason given above, I have introduced two additional lines of my own.

63   *willow-herb*: a perennial of the evening-primrose family. It has long slender leaves and large pink flowers.

63   *dahlia*: it is often associated with funerals or sad events and in this sense occurs frequently in Lorca's work.

65   *fleur-de-lys*: the iris, of which there are many varieties in many different colours.

65   *The clock strikes twelve*: these lines are evidently from 'The Language of the Hours'.

69   *by proxy*: an arrangement whereby one individual is empowered by another to act on his or her behalf. In this case the Nephew will appoint someone to stand in for him at the marriage ceremony.

69   *So what about the nights?*: a good example of the Housekeeper's down-to-earth approach to things. While the other characters indulge in dreams of roses, love, and social status, the Housekeeper has her feet firmly on the ground.

69   *like the whiteness*: a suggestion of Rosita's apprehension in spite of her joy, and of the sad fate that awaits her in the years ahead. In Lorca's work in general, white may signify purity and innocence, as in the case of a bride-to-be, but it also points to the coldness of death and the white sheet in which a corpse was laid out.

71   *In the light of the moon*: see note to p. 25 on the significance of the moon in Lorca's work.

Act Three

73   *A clock strikes six*: clocks or the sound of church bells at specific times are often mentioned in Lorca's plays. See the Commentary, p. xxx–xxxi, on his obsession with passing time.

73   *The clock strikes six again*: this is presumably the same clock. Its mechanism seems to have deteriorated with age and in that respect is symbolic of the house itself, as well as of the people who live in it.

73   *the attic*: the Spanish text has 'the tower'.

73   *Everything is such a burden*: literally, 'We have such a great ruin on top of us'.

73   *your fingertips*: like all Spanish women of her class, the Aunt has devoted herself to the more refined tasks of embroidery and the like, while the Housekeeper has engaged in the more physical demands of cleaning and scrubbing. See too the duties of Poncia and the Servant in *The House of Bernarda Alba*, in contrast to the sewing and embroidery undertaken by Bernarda's daughters.

75   *That's what hurts!*: literally, 'That's the wound!', a typical example of Lorca's concrete images.

75   *my family honour*: made to wait so many years for the Nephew to return, Rosita's plight has become the subject of common gossip, which in turn affects her good name and honour, and, by extension, that of her family. See the Commentary, p. xxxii, on the topic of damaging gossip.

75   *far too old*: if the play covers the period 1890 to 1910, it would mean that in Act Three Rosita is about forty years old and presumably too old for marriage and child bearing, which was such an important factor in a Catholic country.

75   *the power of attorney*: this refers to the marriage 'by proxy' and the authorisation which the Nephew had promised to give to whoever was intended to represent him during the marriage ceremony.

75   *the two jars:* the Spanish word 'orza' means a small earthenware jar. See too the opening scene of *The House of Bernarda Alba*: 'I've opened her sausage-jar!'

77   *Her hair is in ringlets*: the combination of a pink dress
      and a hairstyle which seems more suited to a young girl
      than to a woman who is at least forty years old creates a
      rather grotesque effect.

77   *you can't get through to*: literally, 'and you can't find the
      body'.

77   *an open wound*: a fine example of Lorca's very concrete
      visual imagery. The image of an open wound is one he
      often used to suggest emotional pain, as when Yerma, in
      Act Three, reacts to the First Old Woman's suggestion
      that she should seek comfort in her husband's love:
      'Don't press your finger into that wound in my flesh.'

77   *We have to go with the flow*: literally, 'Let the river take
      us'. See too Adela's bitter attack on one of her sisters in
      Act Two of *The House of Bernarda Alba*: 'Until they are
      suddenly naked and let the current take them'. The
      suggestion is that people are not in control of their lives.

79   *fennel*: a plant of the parsley family with an aniseed
      taste.

79   *a lovely meringue*: literally, 'a snow mountain', a dessert
      made with meringue.

79   *Don Martín*: the school in which Don Martín is a
      teacher was doubtless based on Lorca's memory of the
      College of the Sacred Heart of Jesus in the Placeta de
      Castillejos, near the cathedral in the centre of Granada.
      Despite its name, the school was not a Catholic
      institution. Lorca attended classes there after studying at
      Granada's General and Technical Institute in the
      mornings.

79   *What a nice surprise!*: literally, 'Happy eyes!', the
      equivalent of 'A sight for sore eyes!'

79   *The new house*: if the new house has 'a nice view' it is
      presumably still in the Albaicín, looking over Granada
      and its surrounding area.

79   *rhetoric*: the art of discourse and skill in using language.

79   *I'm disabled*: the real Don Martín was in no way
      disabled. On the contrary, he was very conscious of his
      appearance and extremely upright. But, like Lorca's
      character, he did dye his hair.

81   *Mr Consuegra*: see the Commentary, p. xxix. As well as

being a Latin teacher, Mr Consuegra was a great lover of the bullfight.

81   *Jephthah's Daughter*: see the Commentary, p. xxix. Jephthah was a judge in Israel in the twelfth century BC and a leader of the war against the Ammonites. He was the son of a prostitute and was therefore driven out by his legitimate brothers, but he was subsequently sought by the elders of Gilead in their struggle against the Ammonites. Before the battle, he vowed that he would sacrifice whoever came first out of his house when he returned victorious. The first person to do so proved to be his daughter.

81   *caesura*: the pause between the two halves of a line of verse. In the English translation, the pause occurs after 'horror', in the Spanish original after 'estertor'.

81   *Glucinius*: this may be a character invented by Don Martín. The name does not occur in any reference book.

81   *Isaiah*: a Hebrew prophet who lived in the eighth century BC. Given this fact, it seems even more unlikely that someone with a Roman name – Glucinius – and therefore from a later period, would be associated with him.

83   *St Gertrude the Great*: born in Germany in 1256, she belonged to the Benedictine order and was also a mystic writer. Saint Teresa of Avila took Saint Gertrude as her model and guide, and her writings were revered in Spain. In the Catholic Church the 'novena' is a devotion consisting of prayers or services on nine successive days.

83   *St Anthony's*: this is possibly the convent of San Antón not far from Granada's cathedral. The sound of the bell would certainly be heard high up in the Albaicín.

83   *The Granada Intellectual*: the name seems to be an invention of Lorca's.

83   *Parnassus*: Mount Parnassus, in central Greece, is 8,000 feet in height. In ancient times it was considered to be sacred to Apollo and the nine Muses who presided over poetry, art and science. Apollo was the Greek god of youth, masculine beauty, music, song and prophecy.

85   *hyperbaton*: a transposition of words from their normal order, frequent in poetry.

85   *epinicion*: in Greek poetics the word signifies a victory
      ode.
85   *looks at me daggers*: literally, 'gives me looks as if they
      were two angry cats'.
85   *The Ruins of Palmyra*: the book was published in 1753,
      its author was Robert Wood, a student of ancient history
      and under-secretary from 1756 to 1763 to the then
      Prime Minister, William Pitt. Palmyra is a ruined city in
      the Syrian desert, 150 miles north-east of Damascus.
87   *You've never seen the like!*: in the original a simple ¡ay!,
      an expression of regret or anguish which is the
      equivalent of the rather weak and old-fashioned English
      'Alas!'
87   *Don Rafael Salé*: I have found no evidence that this was
      a real person.
87   *all those priests, all those nuns*: in past times there were
      extremely close links between the wealthy and the
      Catholic Church, hence the representatives of the
      Church at this rich man's funeral. Their presence would
      also, of course, make for a greater show. When a left-
      wing government came into power in 1931, the power of
      the Church and the religious orders was restricted, but
      during and after the Civil War, in which the Left was
      defeated, the Church regained its previous influence and
      was once again supported by the rich.
87   *mumbo-jumbo*: the word 'gori-gori' also occurs at the
      beginning of *The House of Bernarda Alba* when Poncia
      comments disparagingly on the religious service which is
      taking place in the nearby church.
87   *Old Nick's cauldron*: Pedro Botero is the Spanish
      equivalent of the English Old Nick.
87   *a float in the Holy Week procession*: the processions in
      Granada during Holy Week, Semana Santa, are among
      the most impressive in Spain. Images of the Virgin Mary
      and the crucified Christ are placed on large heavy floats
      which are borne on the shoulders of men concealed
      beneath them. The procession is accompanied by others
      dressed in the white robes and conical hats which bring
      to mind the Ku-Klux Klan. Although Lorca's religious
      beliefs were severely tested by his sexual turmoil during

his late teenage years and early twenties, he often turned to religion at critical times in his life, and in 1929, during one of the periods of depression from which he often suffered, he took part in the Holy Week procession organised by the Guild of Saint Mary of the Alhambra, which descended from the Alhambra to the centre of Granada.

89 *The neighbours are sure to be watching*: in *The House of Bernarda Alba* Poncia spies on local people just as they spy on Bernarda's household, eager to seize on any untoward incident that will provide them with food for gossip.

89 *mortgage the house*: the Aunt and Uncle evidently took out a mortgage on the house in order to pay for Rosita's wedding, but, on account of his financial incompetence and the expenditure incurred by his cultivation of flowers, the Uncle was eventually unable to meet the mortgage repayments. The only way for the Aunt to do so is therefore to sell the house and move to a less expensive property.

89 *on your wedding day*: the Aunt is presumably referring to Rosita's future marriage to someone other than the Nephew, for she knows that he is already married.

91 *living outside myself*: the Spanish phrase 'fuera de sí' can also mean 'beside oneself', 'hysterical', but Rosita seems to be saying that she has been living in a fantasy world, in a faraway world of the imagination.

91 *I knew the truth*: yet, for many years, Rosita has denied it. See the Commentary, pp. xlvi, xlix on both her and the Uncle's capacity for self-deception and their escape into a world of illusion.

91 *going to fancy her*: literally, 'going to get his teeth into her'.

93 *a dying wolf*: another good example of Lorca's love of physical, tactile images to suggest emotional pain.

93 *honey-tongued liar*: literally, 'thieving cock-pigeon'.

93 *I am what I am. I can't change*: this is a concept which lies at the heart of Lorca's concept of tragedy. Individuals are what they are and have objectives and aspirations which may be different from those of other

people, who are also what they are, unable to change.
The clash between them inevitably leads to
disappointment, frustration, and, in extreme cases,
catastrophe, as happens in *Blood Wedding, Yerma,* and
The House of Bernarda Alba.

95   *But I shan't be like her*: Rosita is an extremely sad
figure, but by now she also has a steadfast quality which
demands a certain admiration and which also makes her
a more rounded character.

95   *the same time as my husband*: the Housekeeper notes at
the beginning of Act Three that the Uncle died six years
ago, which would have been in 1904. If Act One is set in
1890 and Maria's son is now eighteen, he would have
been born in 1892, in which case his mother succeeded
in finding love not long after the Manolas' meeting with
Rosita in the first act.

97   *your married aunt?*: this is evidently another of the
Manolas who has succeeded in finding love, which
makes Rosita's abandonment all the more touching.

97   *Plaza Nueva*: this square lies at the bottom of the steep
hill, the Cuesta de Gomérez, which climbs from the city
up to the Alhambra.

99   *style of 1912*: yet another confusing date, given that
earlier in this act Rosita enters in a dress *in the style of
1910.*

99   *Don't expose the painful wound*: literally, 'don't remove
the bandage from the sorrow'.

101   *No one will be watching*: literally, 'there'll be no one on
the balconies'.

101   *The door is heard banging . . . the white curtains flutter
in the wind*: the ending of the play has often been
compared to the ending of Chekhov's *The Cherry
Orchard* where the estate has just been sold and the
cherry orchard is to be cut down after the departure of
the family, suggesting the passing of an earlier and now
outdated way of life.

Questions for Further Study

1. What impression do you form of the life-style and activities of the middle-class characters in *Doña Rosita the Spinster*?

2. Discuss the role of women in the kind of society portrayed in *Doña Rosita*.

3. 'Although Rosita's life is wasted, she is in many ways a heroic rather than a pathetic character.' Discuss.

4. To what extent does *Doña Rosita* reveal Lorca's ability as a comic writer?

5. Do you consider that the poetic passages in *Doña Rosita* enhance or detract from the play as a whole?

6. Relate the flower imagery in *Doña Rosita* to the play's principal themes.

7. Discuss the theme of spinsterhood in *Doña Rosita*, including Lorca's attitude to it.

8. Relate the portrayal of social life in *Doña Rosita* to the condition of Spain at the end of the nineteenth century.

9. Do you feel that the shift in mood from the first two acts to the third is successfully achieved?

10. To what extent do many of the characters in *Doña Rosita* escape into a world of fantasy only to be forced in the end to face up to reality?

11. 'Although *Doña Rosita* has a specific Spanish setting, the play has a truly universal appeal.' Illustrate this statement.

12. 'In *Doña Rosita* Lorca makes use of all the different elements of stage performance in order to achieve his ideal of "total theatre".' Discuss.

13. In what ways does Lorca's portrayal of Granada society reflect his own time as well as the past?

14. 'The themes of frustration and passing time were central to both Lorca's life and work.' Relate this statement to *Doña Rosita*.

15. Assess the importance of the theme of honour and reputation in *Doña Rosita*.

16. '*Doña Rosita* reveals Lorca's indebtedness to a variety of theatrical traditions, from puppet play to farce to drawing-room drama.' Discuss.

17. Do you believe that *Doña Rosita* has an appeal for a modern audience?

18. Other than Doña Rosita, which of the play's characters do you find to be most appealing and interesting?

19. 'Although *Doña Rosita* is not a tragedy, it comes very close to being one.' Do you agree?

20. Assess the extent to which Lorca successfully balances laughter and tears in *Doña Rosita*.

21. If you were staging *Doña Rosita*, to what extent would you either follow or update Lorca's original stage directions?

22. Take any scene from *Doña Rosita* and explain how you would direct your actors.

23. Assess the importance of costume and movement in *Doña Rosita*.

GWYNNE EDWARDS is a specialist in Spanish theatre and cinema, until recently Professor of Spanish at the University of Wales, Aberystwyth. His books include: *Lorca: The Theatre Beneath the Sand*; *Lorca: Living in the Theatre*; *Dramatists in Perspective: Spanish Theatre in the Twentieth Century*; *The Discreet Art of Luis Buñuel*; *A Companion to Luis Buñuel*; and *Almodóvar: Labyrinths of Passion*. He has also translated and adapted more than forty plays from Spanish, French and Italian, many of which have been staged at major theatres in Britain and the United States. He has published three collections of Lorca plays with Methuen Drama, together with student editions of *Blood Wedding*, *The House of Bernarda Alba* and *Yerma* and also collections of seventeenth-century Spanish and contemporary Spanish-American plays. Other recent works include two plays adapted from the correspondence and prose writings of Dylan Thomas and the libretto for an opera, *Dylan and Caitlin*.

Methuen Drama Student Editions

Jean Anouilh *Antigone* • John Arden *Serjeant Musgrave's Dance*
Alan Ayckbourn *Confusions* • Aphra Behn *The Rover*
Edward Bond *Lear* • Bertolt Brecht *The Caucasian Chalk Circle*
Life of Galileo • *Mother Courage and her Children*
The Resistible Rise of Arturo Ui • *The Threepenny Opera*
Anton Chekhov *The Cherry Orchard* • *The Seagull* • *Three Sisters*
Uncle Vanya • Caryl Churchill *Serious Money* • *Top Girls*
Shelagh Delaney *A Taste of Honey* • Euripides *Elektra* • *Medea*
Dario Fo *Accidental Death of an Anarchist* • Michael Frayn *Copenhagen*
John Galsworthy *Strife* • Nikolai Gogol *The Government Inspector*
Robert Holman *Across Oka* • Henrik Ibsen *A Doll's House* • *Ghosts*
Hedda Gabler • Charlotte Keatley *My Mother Said I Never Should*
Bernard Kops *Dreams of Anne Frank* • Federico García Lorca
Blood Wedding • *Doña Rosita the Spinster* (bilingual edition) • *The House
of Bernarda Alba* • (bilingual edition) • *Yerma* (bilingual edition) • David
Mamet *Glengarry Glen Ross* • *Oleanna* • Patrick Marber *Closer* • John
Marston *The Malcontent* • Joe Orton *Loot* • Luigi Pirandello *Six
Characters in Search of an Author* • Mark Ravenhill *Shopping and
F***ing* • Willy Russell *Blood Brothers* • *Educating Rita* • Sophocles
Antigone • *Oedipus the King* • Wole Soyinka *Death and the King's
Horseman* • August Strindberg *Miss Julie* • J. M. Synge *The Playboy
of the Western World* • Theatre Workshop *Oh What a Lovely War*
Timberlake Wertenbaker *Our Country's Good* • Arnold Wesker *The
Merchant* • Oscar Wilde *The Importance of Being Earnest* • Tennessee
Williams *A Streetcar Named Desire* • *The Glass Menagerie*